batik

Design, Style & History

batik

Design, Style & History

FIONA KERLOGUE

Featuring selections from the
RUDOLF G. SMEND COLLECTION

Photography by
FULVIO ZANETTINI

and images from the
LEO HAKS PHOTO COLLECTION

Thames & Hudson

Photographs
p. 2: Balinese women carrying
offerings for the temple.
Thilly Weissenborn, ca.1910.
(Leo Haks photo collection,
Amsterdam).
pp. 4–5: Detail of *kain panjang*
from Lasem (see p. 51). *Tulis*,
cotton, natural dyes. 108 x 252 cm.
(Kerlogue collection)
pp. 8–9: Centrefield of a *kain
panjang* made on the north coast
of Java for export to Sumatra.
Tulis, cotton. First half of the
20th century. 108 x 254.5 cm.
(Smend collection)

First published in the United Kingdom in 2004
by Thames & Hudson Ltd, 181A High Holborn,
London WC1V 7QX

www.thamesandhudson.com

First published in the United States of America
in 2004 by Thames & Hudson Inc.,
500 Fifth Avenue, New York, New York 10110

thamesandhudsonusa.com

British Library Cataloguing-in-Publication Data
A catalogue record for this book is available
from the British Library

ISBN 0-500-28477-6
Library of Congress Catalog Card Number:
2003112791

Printed and bound in Singapore

CONTENTS

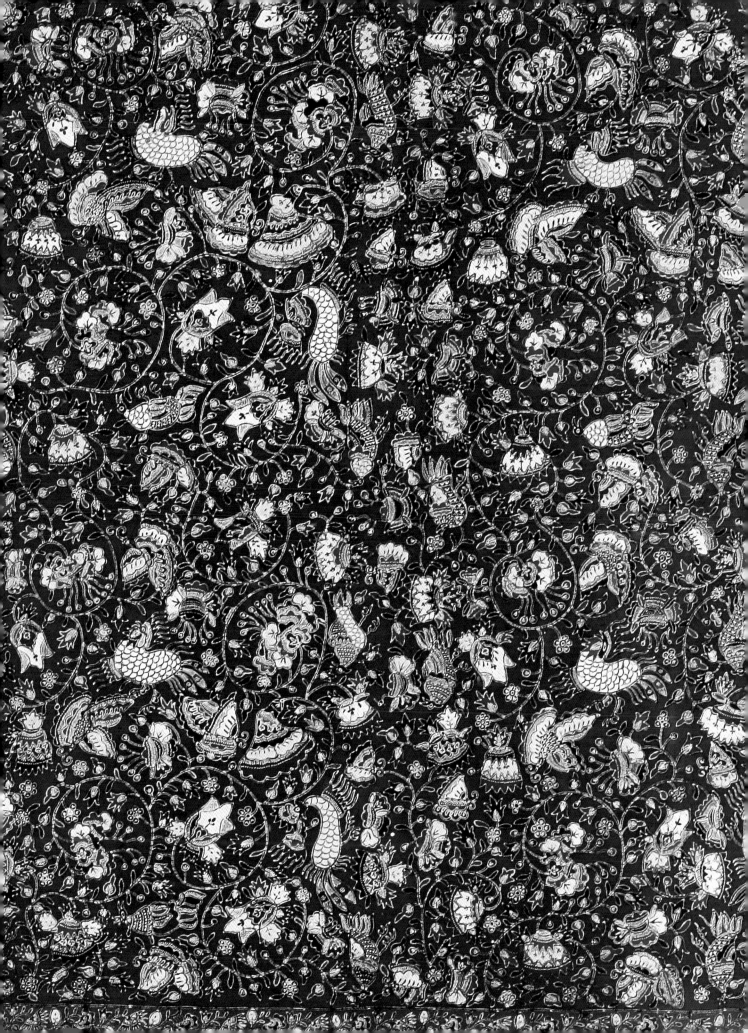

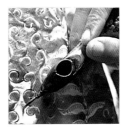

Introduction

Batik has a very special place in the world of textiles. No other cloth in the Indonesian archipelago, perhaps in the whole world, contains so much symbolism and so many meanings. In the philosophy of its colours and designs, and in the way it is made, folded and worn, batik expresses the spirit of the people who make it and wear it and who treasure it as part of their heritage.

Visitors to Java or to any of the other Indonesian islands cannot fail to be struck by the gaily decorated skirt cloths worn by many of the women. Most of these are based on designs derived from those found in traditional batik, Indonesia's most famous textile form. At its simplest, batik is cloth decorated by drawing lines in wax to protect parts of the undyed cloth from colouring in the dyebath. In the marketplace, in the rice fields and in the villages, batik patterns embellish the *sarung* and shawls used for everyday wear by women throughout the archipelago.

But batik is not just worn in the countryside. Cloths made in this way have a strong royal connection, and some designs were reserved for royal use. In the past, many princesses were trained in the skill of applying wax to cloth, much as Western ladies of rank learnt the skills of embroidery. Styles of batik associated with the ruling family and the aristocracy are still worn for ceremonial occasions at the courts of Central Java.

OPPOSITE: Chinese influence is evident in the body of this lively *sarung* from the north coast of Java, with the *banji* (swastika) design and creatures such as the dog-lion depicted in deep red and blue between bands of stylized *parang* motifs. *Tulis*, cotton, natural dyes. 105.5 x 200 cm. (Smend collection)

As king and queen for the day, brides and bridegrooms also wear costumes which echo the clothing of the nobility.

Batiks also have a special place in rituals performed within the community: to protect the wearer from harm, to symbolize the relationship between two families newly joined through a wedding, to heal the sick or to mark off sacred space. Batiks from Java became incorporated into rituals in many of the outer islands of Indonesia as well as within Java itself.

Nowadays, much of the batik used in Indonesia is produced in factories in Java, whether the wax is applied by printing or drawn on by hand. In some enterprises, women may sit in a group of six or seven around an oil stove, scooping out hot wax with which to draw the patterns onto the cloth. Some may work for a daily wage, others are paid by the piece. Some businesses operate a different system whereby women work at home. They collect bundles of cloth from the entrepreneur's workshop to work on at their own pace and in the company of friends and family. The dyeing is nowadays most likely to be carried out by men at the workshop. In rare instances, a third type of system operates where a few highly skilled batik makers may undertake the whole process within one family. It is at these specialist workshops that the highest quality batik is produced.

What marks out a piece of batik as being particularly fine? Good quality batik should be waxed on both sides of the cloth, with the design as bright and clear on one side as it is on the other. Indonesian women looking to buy commonly press the cloth to their faces and breathe in the fragrant aroma of the wax, which is usually still strong in a piece of batik waxed by hand. Particularly fine pieces will often have elements worked with fine delicate lines. If there is a large background area of white or of one colour, this should be clear, with no spills or smudges. In general, the spidery lines characteristic of African batik are absent in good quality Javanese cloths, as they are evidence that the wax has cracked and the dye has seeped in. There are a few exceptions, where the wax has been deliberately cracked to produce a marbled effect, but accidental cracking is frowned upon.

Javanese purchasers of batik may spend a considerable amount of money on one piece, especially if it is to be used as a gift. Batik cloths presented to a girl on her wedding day may never be worn. Often they are folded away and eventually become heirlooms to be handed down from generation to

This vibrant *sarung* was probably made in Madura, though it was collected in Jambi. The background filling design is known as *carcena*, a corruption of *pacar cina*, meaning 'Chinese sweetheart', the name of a flower. *Tulis*, cotton. 107 x 202 cm. (Kerlogue collection)

generation. These expensive pieces are usually commissioned from an expert maker and decorated with motifs imbued with auspicious significance.

Batik has other uses besides clothing; as flags and banners or wall hangings, for example. In the last century batik began to be used for tablecloths, curtains and other soft furnishings. In addition, the production of batik paintings was started, initially using the traditional techniques but later incorporating methods such as applying the dye with an aerosol spray or painting it on by hand. This gave rise to a very different kind of work, sometimes bearing no resemblance at all to traditional batik. Artists with an art school background now tend to draw their inspiration from the fine arts rather than from the motifs found on traditional *sarung*.

In Indonesia the art of batik has developed a further significance in recent times as an expression of regional and national identity. It is worn by politicians at regional and local levels, by students on their graduation day, by hotel staff and tourist guides and by civil servants as part of their uniform. Batik is made in many other countries all over the world. But it is in Indonesia that it has become an expression of local pride and an essential symbol of the nation.

The Sultan of Surakarta with his wife and daughter. Photographer unknown, 1945. (Leo Haks photo collection, Amsterdam)

FOLLOWING PAGES: *Dlorong bulat galaran*. The colours in this delicately drawn *sarung* reflect the taste of the north coast of Java. The triangular *pucuk rebung* of traditional *kepala* panels have been replaced with diagonal bands, and the daisies reflect a strong European influence. *Tulis*, cotton. Signed Ny Lie Boe In, Kudus, 1930s. 106 x 207.5 cm. (Smend collection)

Origins

The term 'batik' is used generally to refer to cloth which has been decorated by a wax resist technique. A pattern is applied in hot wax onto a piece of undyed cloth, usually cotton. When the cloth is later dyed, those parts which have been treated with wax will not take up the dye, and when the wax is removed a pattern of white lines will be left. This process can be repeated with a number of subsequent waxings and dyebaths, leaving a complex pattern of motifs in a variety of colours.

How long this method of decorating cloth has been practised is not known. The technique has been recorded in many countries throughout the world, from Peru to Indonesia, from Turkestan to China. Fragments of fabric decorated with a resist technique have been found in tombs in China dating back to the sixth century, and by the eighth century the wax resist technique seems to have spread to Japan. But it is by its Indonesian name, 'batik', that the process is best known, and most people agree that it is in Indonesia that the skill of batik making has reached the highest level of artistry.

The word 'batik'

The earliest known written reference to 'batik' is almost certainly in a Dutch bill of lading of 1641 connected

OPPOSITE: Copper printing stamps (*cap*) were introduced around the middle of the 19th century to speed up production in commercial workshops. Some of the stamps are works of art in themselves. 16.5 x 18 cm. (Smend collection)

with a shipment of cargo from Batavia in Java to Bengkulu on the west coast of Sumatra. Whether the word was used to refer to precisely what we call 'batik' today is uncertain. Even now, the word is applied quite loosely by many Indonesians to any form of patterned cloth. There may well have been cloth patterned using the wax resist technique before the word was applied to it, so batik may have existed before the word we now use to describe it. For example, there are references to cloth which has been drawn on, or painted on, in Javanese texts dating back to the twelfth century. Whether these are early references to batik will probably never be known, and allusions to the writing or drawing of designs could equally well refer to the drawing on of gold or the painting of dyestuffs directly onto the cloth. Linguistic evidence is inconclusive and for evidence of the origins of batik we must look elsewhere.

Statuary

In examining archaeological remains, many writers have pointed out that some of the patterns found in present-day batik appear in early stone carvings. Panels of decorative bas-reliefs at the tenth-century temple complex, Loro Jonggrang, at Prambanan near Yogyakarta in Central Java, are carved with motifs comparable with some present-day batik designs. There are also a number of statues dating from this period in which the figures wear costumes with design elements which appear to resemble those we find in batik. However, the designs on these monuments could equally well be representing the patterns found on brocade or *songket*, which contain very similar forms. Another type of cloth originating in Indonesia which seems to have existed around that time is *ikat*, a type of textile where the threads are tied before they are dyed and woven. Similar design motifs appear on many *ikat* cloths which survive from the nineteenth century, and so the idea that the textiles depicted in the statuary are made by the *ikat* process rather than batik cannot be dismissed.

Overseas connections

In the textile practices of traditional societies both within the Indonesian archipelago and among its neighbours, techniques are used which some see as the forerunners of the batik of present-day Indonesia. In the mountains of southwest China,

North Vietnam and the Golden Triangle between Laos, Thailand and Burma, the Hmong peoples make intricate patterns on their hemp or cotton skirts using a copper tool and beeswax. The wax is applied onto the undyed cloth which is then soaked in an infusion of indigo, producing geometric patterns in white against a deep saturated blue. If the technique spread from China with these people, it may well have spread in a similar way to the archipelago.

In India, batik takes a rather different form. Cloths have been exported from there to Indonesia for centuries, many of them patterned with a resist dye technique. One method was to apply the wax with a *kalam*, a metal spike with a bulb at one end around which twine was wound. This acted as a reservoir for the hot wax before it ran down onto the cloth. Another technique was to stamp wax or some other resist substance onto the cloth with wooden blocks. Resist-dyed textiles from India have been imported into Indonesia from at least the thirteenth century and probably much earlier, and it may well be that some aspects of the technique were adopted and then adapted locally.

The Indonesian archipelago

However, there is no reason to suppose that the technique of batik making did not evolve in several different places simultaneously. In Indonesia itself, cloths dyed using simple resist materials other than wax have been recorded in several of the islands. These other examples include the *sarita* cloths of Sulawesi, in which rice paste resist techniques are practised to decorate cloths used as ritual objects by the Torajans. Another example is the *kain simbut* of West Java, where rice paste was employed to decorate cloths used for similar purposes. The tools used ranged from a palm-leaf bag to a bamboo quill. These instances are widely regarded as vestiges of forerunners of modern batik, from which wax batik may have derived, and this theory seems plausible. It is possible that the *canting*, the copper tool used nowadays in Java to draw the hot wax onto the surface of the cloth, was not invented until the eighteenth century. As far as is known, the word is not found in Old or Middle Javanese.

The likeliest source of present-day batik practices is a combination of locally existing textile techniques with a range

Water-colour paintings showing the application of wax by means of the *canting* (LEFT); with the copper stamp known as the *cap* (CENTRE); and the dyeing process (RIGHT). The division of labour along gender lines is typical of small-scale production today. Before the introduction of synthetic dyes, women would have performed most of the dyeing.

of innovations introduced by practitioners over the centuries. Some of these may have been based on ideas and materials brought by settlers and visitors from other parts of the archipelago, some from traders and immigrants from overseas, and some were probably the result of inventive exploration by enterprising women, always looking for ways of improving the quality of their art and increasing the variety of decoration by adapting their production methods. In the same way, motifs found on imported textiles were often incorporated into the design fields of Indonesian cloths.

Materials

The earliest batiks were probably produced using cloth made of fibres from native plants such as ramie or abaca, long before recorded history. Cotton was almost certainly introduced from India at some point during the first millennium; by the ninth century it was being sent to China from Sumatra as an exotic fabric. For the batik made today in Indonesia, finely woven cotton fabric of the highest quality is usually employed, but it is possible to use handwoven cloth made of handspun threads. Fabric made this way, from cotton grown in the village fields,

is still used for batik making in Kerek near Tuban in the east of Java, and it is thought that batiks from this area resemble most closely the batiks produced before factory-made cloth was brought into play. Not only is the fabric produced locally, but the most important dye, indigo, is also grown around the villages, as it would have been over much of the region at one time.

The dye most widely used before the introduction of synthetic dyes was indigo, which gives a rich blue colour. Some writers suggest that indigo may have been introduced to Indonesia from India, but a variety of indigo was found in Sumatra which was unknown to English botanists in 1780, and which is probably a native variety. Indigo is a vat dye, for which the dye must be fermented with other materials in order to make it soluble. The colour only develops when the cloth is later hung out in the air and the dye is oxidized. Repeated immersions are needed to make a deep colour, and the process may last for a week or more. The ingredients used in an indigo vat vary; a report of batik making in Java published early in the twentieth century mentioned an enormous range of ingredients, from cane sugar and molasses to *mengkudu* fruit and chicken bones. Some of these ingredients are essential to the process, while others have a more symbolic function, often to drive away evil spirits. All were available locally, so that there is no reason to suppose that the art of indigo dyeing itself was introduced from outside Indonesia.

For red, many different materials were used, including sappanwood and stick lac, a residue left by a tiny insect in the bark of certain trees. But the dyestuff most commonly used was the bark of the root of the *mengkudu* tree. In order for the dye from this plant to be fast, a mordant was needed, that is, a substance which would bind the colour to the cloth. The most usual source was a plant known in Java as *jirak*, rich in aluminium salts. Much skill and knowledge was needed in judging the temperatures and proportions required to obtain good results from these materials, which continued in use well into the twentieth century.

Other important natural dyestuffs included a number of wood dyes which, in addition to giving a yellow or brown colour, acted as mordants. Those used in Sumatran batik differed from those used in Java, which lends weight to the argument that batik making was not necessarily a Javanese craft transplanted to Sumatra, but one which grew up there as a separate tradition.

The waxes used in batik making consist of mixtures of substances: tree resins and gums, beeswax and, in the past, a range of animal fats, especially from buffalo and elephant. In the dense tropical jungles of Indonesia, all these materials were available locally. Traders have exchanged iron goods, salt, rice and textiles with the forest dwellers to obtain such forest products since at least the thirteenth century and probably much earlier. It seems that in the Indonesian archipelago all the ingredients needed for batik making have existed for many centuries.

Court and countryside

By the eighteenth century, batik was a central element in court dress for the royal courts at Solo and Yogyakarta. Certain designs were allowed to be worn only by members of the royal family. In 1811 a treaty between Sir Stamford Raffles, the new British Lieutenant Governor of Java, and Sultan Hamengkubuwono II in Yogyakarta stated that 'His Highness engages not to prohibit to any class of his subjects the use of

any particular article or wearing-apparel, ornament or luxury, except the cloth called *parang roosa* and *sawat*, which from time immemorial have been appropriated to the Royal person'. The reference to 'time immemorial' is certainly an exaggeration, and probably means that the prohibition had applied since the founding of the Yogyakarta court as a separate sultanate from that of Solo in the previous century. How long the art of batik had been practised at court is uncertain.

Although batik work is thought to have been undertaken in the countryside in one form or another for many centuries, most peasants in the past would have worn very plain cloths, undyed or decorated very simply. The use of batik embellishment was probably at one time reserved for those in high positions in the village or for ritual occasions. Most scholars now believe that artisans skilled in the production of such cloths were brought to the court from the countryside. Court patronage operated in this way for many other craftworkers, especially those producing articles believed to contain sacred powers. This included special smiths skilled in the making of damascene blades for the *kris*, the mystical dagger worn by men of status, and master carvers who fashioned the hilts and sheaths associated with them and of almost equal power. These artisans lived in the buildings surrounding the *kraton* (palace), and were employed and protected by the ruler.

At the same time, batik production continued in the countryside, where it also carried symbolic resonance. In many parts of Indonesia, the beliefs associated with the power of the dye vat and the meanings which underlie many of the traditional motifs, passed down the generations and imbued with significance, still continue to this day.

Printing

Batik waxed by hand with a *canting* is known as 'batik tulis'. But not all batik is made in this way. In the mid-nineteenth century a copper stamp, or *cap*, used to apply the wax to the cloth, was developed in Java. The development of the *cap*, made of copper strips usually formed in a rectangular frame, was probably inspired by the wooden stamps which were in use in other aspects of textile production. Wooden stamps had long been used in India for the application of mordants, dyes and resist substances, and there is evidence of their use in Indonesia. Raffles referred to the use of wood blocks in the early nineteenth century in Java where the cloths were 'stamped as in India' in imitation of Indian cloths. They were used around the same period in Palembang in Sumatra for the block printing of chintzes, and waxing blocks were found in the late nineteenth century in Aceh, North Sumatra. Many of the old heirloom textiles found in Jambi in Central Sumatra have their patterns stamped on them, and although some of these may have been imported from overseas, it seems that a sizeable proportion of them represent the remains of Indonesian textile production based on block printing. Old wooden printing blocks are still to be found in Palembang. While some were certainly used for the application of gold dust to textiles, others may well have been used for different aspects of textile production. It now seems likely that some of these wooden blocks were the forerunners of the copper *cap*.

The introduction of the *cap* had a significant effect on batik production. Entrepreneurs, many of Arab and Chinese origin, began to establish printing workshops, particularly along the north coast of Java. While the application of wax onto cloth with a *canting* had been almost exclusively a task reserved for women, as it is today, increasingly men became involved. In the batik factories the work was heavier and more physically demanding, opening up a role for men. With the emergence of *cap* production, the ritual and symbolic significance which had been a central part of home batik production declined, and commercial factors came to the fore.

One of the results of the commercialization of batik production was an increased merging of regional styles. With the connection between meaning and motif further weakened, demand came to be shaped by taste and fashion rather than by traditional understandings of meaning. At the same time, the proportion of customers who could afford to buy hand-drawn batik declined so that printed and imitation batiks came to dominate the market. Much of this production was screen-printed, and involved no resist element at all.

However, some workshops still exist where *batik tulis* is undertaken in the age-old way. The finely worked cloths are highly prized. They may be worn on special occasions or presented as gifts at weddings. Many Javanese ladies keep a collection of batiks, some of which they have acquired themselves, while others may be heirlooms, passed down from generation to generation. Some of these may never have been worn, but are carefully stored, brought out only to show to special friends and guests, a source of pride and treasured testimony of the owner's heritage.

Cloths kept as heirlooms in the upriver regions of Central Sumatra provide evidence as to what type of textiles were being produced with wooden blocks in the 19th century. Mordant and resist printing, cotton. Jambi, Sumatra. 90.5 x 201 cm. (Smend collection)

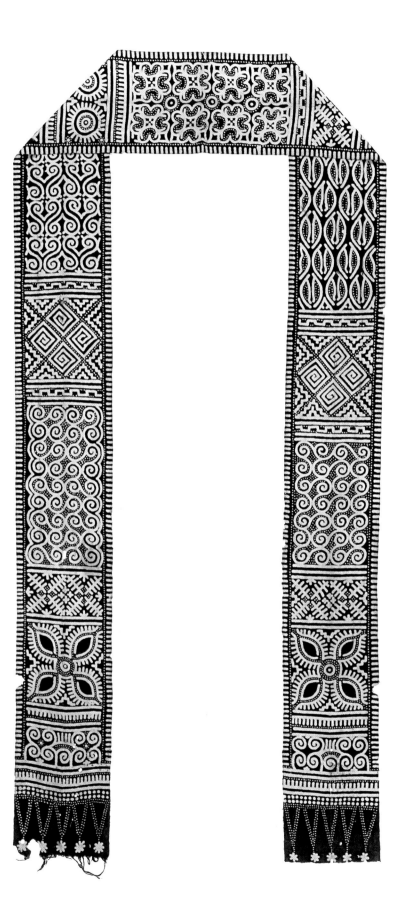

LEFT AND ABOVE (detail): The people of Tana Toraja in Sulawesi used a variety of techniques in producing their textiles, including rice paste and wax resist as well as printing. The narrow *sarita* cloths may have been made in imitation of imported Indian textiles. The Dutch exported their own versions to Sulawesi between 1880 and 1930. *Sarita* cloths were highly valued in South Sulawesi where they were used ceremonially for wrapping around house poles and effigies, as banners, or worn around the head or waist by men on ritual occasions. The designs relate to status, well-being and prosperity. *Tulis*, homespun handwoven cotton, natural dye. Early 20th century. 21 x 373 cm. (Smend collection)

The pattern on this cloth (SEE
DETAIL ON PAGE 55) from the Kerek
district, near Tuban, has been
produced by applying wax dots
onto a cloth woven in black and
white stripes. The cloth was then
immersed in a red dyebath, leaving
a simple geometrical design. This
type of method may have been a
forerunner of the modern practice
of batik making. *Tulis*, cotton.
Margorejo. 51 x 200 cm.
(Kerlogue collection)

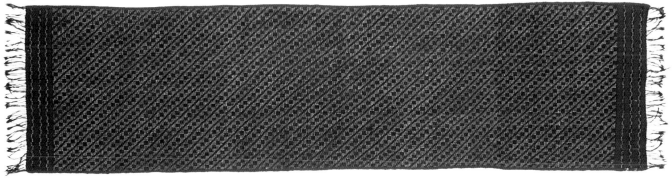

Kain simbut were made and used
as ceremonial cloths in parts of
West Java. They were decorated
by means of a paste resist made
from glutinous rice. Only mature
women could apply the design,
which included symbols of the
cosmos. The central lozenge is
typical. The cloths were used to
repel evil influences at life
crisis ceremonies such as birth,
circumcision or tooth-filing.
Cotton. Rangkasbiting, West Java,
early 20th century. 95 x 195 cm.
(Inv. no. 26131, Wereldmuseum,
Rotterdam)

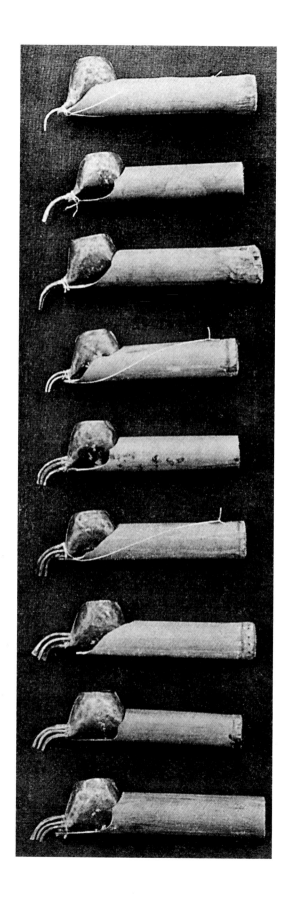

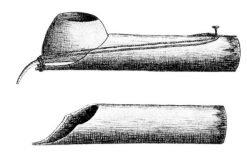

LEFT AND ABOVE: The tool used for applying hot wax by hand, the *canting*, is made of two elements: a copper bowl with a spout, and a bamboo holder into which the copper part is inserted. *Canting* with fine spouts are used for the most delicate lines, while a wide spout allows the wax to flow quickly over background areas. Rosettes of five or seven dots are made with a *canting* which has multiple spouts.
(Jasper and Pirngadie, fig. 16)

An early 19th-century tool-maker in Yogyakarta fitting the copper basin of the *canting* into the hollow bamboo handle.
(Jasper and Pirngadie, fig. 15)

LEFT: The first lines to be drawn are the main outlines of the design (TOP); later parts of the background may be filled in with a darker wax (MIDDLE); after the first dyebath the wax may be removed and a further layer applied (BOTTOM).

ABOVE: Melting off the wax after dyeing. The woman on the right has a large scoop with which she skims the molten wax from the surface of the water.
(Jasper and Pirngadie, fig. 44)

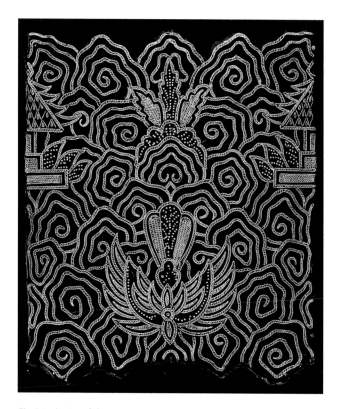

The introduction of the *cap* speeded up production of batik, especially along the north coast and in Batavia. Designs formerly associated with the royal courts became available to the population at large. This one combines the rock motifs associated with the Cirebon court with the *sawat* motif, consisting of a pair of wings and tail representing Garuda. 17 x 20 cm. (Smend collection)

The waxing-stamp or *cap* is made of strips of copper plate twisted to the shape of the design and fixed vertically within a frame attached to a handle. (Jasper and Pirngadie, fig. 17)

This wooden printing stamp from Sumatra may have been used to apply a resist, mordant, gold leaf or dyes to *sarungs* decorated locally. (Kerlogue collection)

ABOVE: *Cap* have been made in much the same way for more than 150 years. On the left a length of copper is being cut from a strip, ready to be folded to form part of the design. On the right another man assembles the sections in the shape of the motif. (Jasper and Pirngadie, fig. 18)

BELOW: A *cap* workshop in Solo (Surakarta) in the early years of the 20th century. The hot wax is in a tray on a circular stove behind and to the side of the worker. He lays his stamp on a wax-soaked pad of jute in the tray, so that it picks up just enough wax to transfer a neat impression of the pattern onto the cloth.
(Jasper and Pirngadie, fig. 54)

ABOVE: The stamping of wax onto the cloth using a *cap* is usually undertaken by men in a semi-industrial setting.

FOLLOWING PAGES: Peranakan-style *kain panjang* with *booh* (bow) border, which is composed of the same pattern all the way round. Although the design in the border echoes the structure of the flowers in the *badan*, it was probably produced beforehand at a different workshop, the cloth having been sold on as a *kain blangko*.
Tulis, cotton. Lasem, ca. 1940.
104.5 x 252 cm. (Smend collection)

2

Regional Traditions

Batik is produced in a great many different parts of Java as well as on other Indonesian islands. In cases where the same motifs appear in batik from more than one place, the interpretations of those motifs may vary. There seems to be a bewildering variety of names and patterns, and it is often hard to know where a particular piece of batik came from. However, in the past there were fairly distinct differences in appearance between the batiks from the various districts where it was made. This resulted partly from differences in materials used, partly from variations in production methods and partly from differing cultural patterns and beliefs. The uses to which batik was put also varied from one place to another, and cloths appropriate for people of different ranks in society also varied from place to place.

The principalities

The most well known batiks from Java are probably the batiks from the courts. At the court of Mataram, based in Surakarta in Central Java until the mid-eighteenth century, certain designs were set apart for use by the royal family. These were almost certainly believed to

OPPOSITE: Jambi batik differs markedly from that of Java. This mythological creature, standing out in gold against a midnight-blue ground, appears nowhere else in the batik of Indonesia. The design of the borders, the spangled effect and the discrete filling motifs are all characteristic of the classical style of Jambi. *Tulis*, cotton, natural dyes. Early 20th century. 119 x 198 cm. (Kerlogue collection)

have talismanic qualities, as was the case, for example, with some of the motifs carved in the hilt of the *kris* (dagger), one of the elements in the regalia of the sultan. Mystical meanings associated with such objects related to the power with which they were imbued; allowing others to use these designs would weaken the sultan's hold on power. The sultan, as the still centre of the universe, must be protected both physically and spiritually in order that his kingdom remains safe and fertile. Thus many of the palace motifs express notions of power, fertility and the spiritual qualities embodied by the person of the sultan.

In 1769, 1784 and 1790, royal decrees were published which laid down precisely which patterns were *larangan* (forbidden). The two cloths which Raffles brought back from Java to England and which are now in the British Museum, were both *larangan* types, and it is likely that they were a gift from the court. In 1816 one of Stamford Raffles' lieutenants, Captain Thomas Travers, recorded in his journal that he had received from a Yogyakarta prince the gift of a batik cloth 'such as is worn by the royal family'.

The court batik of Mataram was characterized by a narrow colour range dominated by the deep blue produced by

Daughters of the Emperor of Solo wearing *kain* decorated with one of the *parang* group of motifs associated with the royal courts of Central Java. Isidore van Kinsbergen, 1865–68. (Yu-Chee Chong Fine Art, London)

repeated immersion of the cloth in an indigo dyebath, and a sombre brown known as *soga*, produced by dyes from the barks of trees. Other materials were needed as fixing agents or as modifiers of the various tones. These characteristic colours continued to dominate Central Javanese court batik, though a distinction did develop between the batik of Yogyakarta and the batik of Surakarta (the present-day city of Solo).

In the mid-eighteenth century, when the then ruler of Mataram died, a bitter quarrel over the succession had divided the family. The result was a split into two principalities, one based in Surakarta, and the other in Yogyakarta. The new ruler of Yogyakarta was determined that his court should continue the Mataram traditions, but he distinguished his own palace from the one at Surakarta in a number of ways. He retained the batik designs reserved for court use, but the background colour at his court was to be white as opposed to the creamy beige of Surakarta, and the diagonal slant of the *parang rusak* design was to run in the opposite direction to that of Surakarta. Early batiks from these two batik-making centres can thus be distinguished by these characteristics, but many makers today are either unaware of or unconcerned by these traditions, and it is not possible to use these criteria for identification of present-day batiks.

The batik of the courts differed from batik made for other sections of the population. Outside the courts, the two main types were the batik produced for the *saudagar*, or trading classes, and the batik of the common people.

Cirebon

As well as the courts of Central Java, there was a sultanate centred on Cirebon for many centuries, where there were several palaces. Here the nobility used their own styles of batik, which differed from those at the Mataram court. Cirebon's location on the north coast of the island, and its trade and other connections with the world beyond, have led to a number of elements being assimilated into their batik designs. These include influences from China, from the Arab Islamic world and from Hindu mythology.

The most well known of Cirebon's batik motifs, and the one which has now come to be used as an expression of Cirebon identity, is the *megamendung* or 'cloud' motif. This is

One characteristic group of Cirebon designs represents the royal gardens where the ruler would meditate. Pavilions and artificial mountains are typical of such gardens, reflected in the rocky landscape depicted on this cloth. The wings on top of the mounds suggest the elevated state which the meditator reaches to release himself from the mundane world. *Taman Arum Sunyaragi. Tulis*, cotton. Cirebon. 105 x 234.5 cm. (DETAIL OF CLOTH ILLUSTRATED ON PAGE 40) (Smend collection)

derived directly from Chinese iconography, and consists of repeated curvilinear bands of one colour, usually blue, in gradations of tones from light to dark. The greater the number of bands, the more dyebaths the cloth has undergone, and the more valuable the cloth.

Another motif identified exclusively with Cirebon in the past was the *peksinagaliman*, a mythical beast made up of elements from the *peksi*, a phoenix-like bird, the *naga*, or serpent, and the *liman*, or elephant. It has been suggested that this creature represents a synthesis of Persian, Hindu and Islamic elements, and thus symbolizes the peaceful coexistence of different cultures living in harmony.

Nowadays Cirebon is a centre for batik manufacture on a large scale, and the traditional designs form only a tiny proportion of the output of these manufactories, or workshops.

Indramayu

Indramayu was once an important port for exporting produce from the Javanese hinterland. The batiks of Indramayu have been less affected by commercialism than those of neighbouring Cirebon, where many batik makers send their cloths for dyeing. The traditional palette of Indramayu is restricted to blue and brown, with the designs usually set against a creamy ground. The large Chinese community has left its mark on the

designs, which often feature phoenixes and other elements of *lokcan* style. '*Lokcan*', a word which literally means 'blue silk', is the name given to a style characterized by birds and animal motifs based on Chinese imagery. The *banji*, or swastika, is a filling motif often used in Indramayu which derives from Chinese iconography. Another characteristic which Indramayu cloths share with older batiks from Cirebon and other north coast centres is the use of the *complongan*. The *complongan* is a piece of wood into which are fixed a large number of pins used to pierce the wax covering the background areas. This results in a sprinkling of tiny dots in the white background where the dye has been able to penetrate. Another feature which characterizes the work of Indramayu is that shawls (*selendang*) are nowadays almost invariably edged with a row of narrow parallel lines and finished with a fringe.

Pekalongan

The story of batik in Pekalongan differs somewhat from the older traditions of the court centres of Yogyakarta, Surakarta (Solo) and Cirebon. The town of Pekalongan was founded comparatively recently, in the seventeenth century, and right from the start it attracted large numbers of immigrants. The city grew quickly, its success based on trade and agriculture, and its wealthy inhabitants developed a taste for luxury textiles. Some were imported, but Pekalongan produced finely woven fabric of its own.

By the nineteenth century, immigrant Arabs had established a thriving trade in batiks in Pekalongan. They supplied both Javanese and European women with the materials for production, and bought the finished cloths from them for marketing in areas where batik production had declined. As European styles grew in popularity and the industry expanded, European entrepreneurs set up their own workshops. Pekalongan was one of the first areas to take up the use of the copper wax stamp, the *cap*, which speeded up production enormously. The city became a centre for commercial production and for the batik trade, supplying a market within Java and to the outer islands of the Dutch East Indies.

Pekalongan is now famous for the European styles of the *sarung* produced there in the late nineteenth and early twentieth centuries, known as 'Batik Nonya'. Many of these were characterized by bunches of flowers, known as *buketan* (from 'bouquet'), in the centre panel. Others depicted characters from European fairy tales and other Western motifs. The cloths are also well known for their bright and varied palette, a result of the early adoption of artificial dyes. Many batiks echoed the colours of the ceramics favoured by the Straits Chinese: greens, pinks, yellows and blues. Today, Pekalongan produces huge quantities of household textiles decorated with batik motifs, much of it for the export market. These are still brightly coloured, but the *sarungs* and *selendangs* made in Pekalongan today are more likely to be finished with a final brown dyebath of *soga*, to suit the Javanese character of the current market in Indonesia.

Lasem

The roofs of the houses and courtyards of the town of Lasem reveal its unmistakably Chinese character and the batik, too, shows clearly the influence of settlers from China. In the nineteenth century the town was famous for the bright reds of its batik, and even today, some batiks are dyed first in Lasem, where those parts which have been dyed red are then irotected with wax before the cloths are sent further afield for the other parts to be dyed in the remaining colours required. Such cloths are known as *tiga negeri*, or 'three-country' batik, as it was common for three different places to be involved in its manufacture.

Many of the batik enterprises in Lasem are still owned by families of Chinese origin, who employ Javanese women as outworkers to carry out the waxing. The dyeing process, still a closely guarded secret, is carried out at the entrepreneur's own premises and under his guidance. The designs produced in Lasem are now as varied as elsewhere in Java, depending on the demand from cities such as Surabaya, where much of the product is sold. It is nowadays rare to find the famous 'laseman' cloth, characterized by *lokcan* patterns of phoenixes, dog-lions or other mythical beasts in red on a white ground.

Kerek

In the Kerek district near Tuban in northeastern Java, some batik production continues much as it must have done in previous centuries. Batik is drawn on cloth woven in the village using thread handspun from locally grown cotton. The dyeing is normally undertaken only by women of mature years who have inherited the specialist knowledge required. The designs on Kerek batik are produced using two main colours, traditionally made from indigo (for blue), which is still grown locally, and *mengkudu* (for red), the latter purchased in the market. Nowadays aniline dyes are used for much of the dyeing, though the use of natural dyes is being revived.

Designs fall into three main types. In one, the centrefield of the cloth is patterned with flowers and birds set against a background of leaf and tendril patterns. Cloths of this type are used as daily wear. The second type consists of two symmetrical stylized flower motifs, usually with six or eight petals, which alternate in regular rows. It is these cloths which are employed during ceremonial occasions.

As well as these batik cloths, Kerek produces a simpler style of batik, which may represent an earlier form. This batik, known as *batik lurik*, is produced by making patterns of dots on a striped or checked cloth, woven in blue-black and white. After the waxing, the cloth is dyed red. When the wax is finally removed, a pattern of white dots is left against the red-and-black background. This type of batik could be produced with the simplest of tools and may represent one of the forerunners of the fine intricate batik work produced in the last century.

Juana

In Juana, Rembang and Pati in northern Java, batik designs on silk *selendang* were once produced for export to Sumatra and Bali, where they were important elements in local costume. The *shantung* silk used was imported from China. During the Depression of the 1930s and the political upheavals which followed it, trade was disrupted and production died out. Most designs were *lokcan* in two shades of blue or brown.

Madura

In Madura in the early years of the twentieth century, several methods were used to produce different colours, but in general cloths fell into two types. One was similar to the colour scheme of Central Javanese court styles (deep blue, brown and cream or white) while the other resembled the brighter and more varied styles of the north coast of Java. In

Madura, this second type was famous for a fiery red produced from a mixture of the bark of the *mengkudu* tree, a mordant obtained from *jirak*, and the brown dye known as *soga*. Although this dye mixture was also used in parts of Java, in Madura a different technique was used and this resulted in a rich ruddy colour which is nowadays achieved with chemical dyes. Some Madurese batik makers were very skilled, and could rival the batik makers of Java in their intricate and delicate work. Madura still produces very fine batik, especially from the Tanjungbumi district.

One of the characteristics of Madurese batik is the range of filling designs, or *guri*. Very often a Madurese cloth will have a number of different filling designs, contained in circles or other shapes. Where one filling design is dominant it will be this, rather than the foreground motif, which gives the cloth its name. In Madura, grandparents present their children with a special baby-carrying cloth, or *ban-ban*, on the occasion of the birth of a grandchild. The distinctive design of these cloths is reminiscent of the design on Kashmiri woven shawls, with panels at each end containing *koni* motifs, known in Britain as the paisley motif.

Jambi

The still-thriving batik tradition of Jambi in Sumatra has from time to time borrowed elements from external sources such as Java, India and Turkey. However, the predominantly Malay people of Jambi have incorporated these features into designs which are characteristically Malay in their symmetrical half-drop designs and predominantly floral motifs. Although in the past many writers have described Jambi batiks as having a characteristic red colour, by the early twentieth century most batik produced in Jambi was dyed in a combination of deep blue and golden yellow. The impression of shimmering gold was produced by dyeing the whole cloth in an infusion of wood chips from the *lembato* tree before the cloth was waxed. After the indigo bath, the wax was cracked and the cloth immersed in a warm brown dyebath made from the bark of another tree found locally, the *marelang*. The result was a marbling in the yellow panels around the edges of the cloth which from a distance made the cloths seem as if they had been embroidered in gold. The most prestigious cloths in Malay societies are *songket*, silk brocades interwoven with gold thread, and most batik designs from Jambi echo the designs of their brocades.

Other centres

Other centres in Java have long-standing traditions of batik production. In Central Java, the towns of Banyumas and Kudus are famous for their distinctive styles. In Banyumas, the warm brown *soga* colour has a rich orange tinge to it. Some noble families were involved in batik production, and the designs often relate to those of the courts of Solo (Surakarta) and Yogyakarta. There were also Arab and Chinese producers and some of Dutch descent. Kudus is famous for the intricacy of its background motifs, or *isen*. In East Java, Gresik was once a major batik centre, much of its output produced for the Sumatran market. Some of the dyes were painted on, a method which helped to speed up the process. Styles were geared towards the market, so there are often resemblances between the batik of Jambi and Gresik. However, Gresik batiks are more likely to have been stamped.

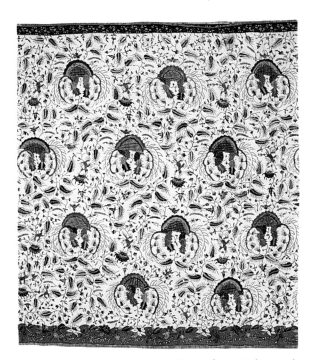

Batik from Java's north coast often combined elements from several sources. In this exquisitely worked piece the shape of the wings of Garuda can be made out, a design usually associated with the Central Javanese court tradition. The borders reflect European influence, however. To produce such fine lines the maker had to wax around the slender lines, a task which required a high level of craftsmanship. *Tulis*, cotton. 107 x 192 cm. (Kerlogue collection)

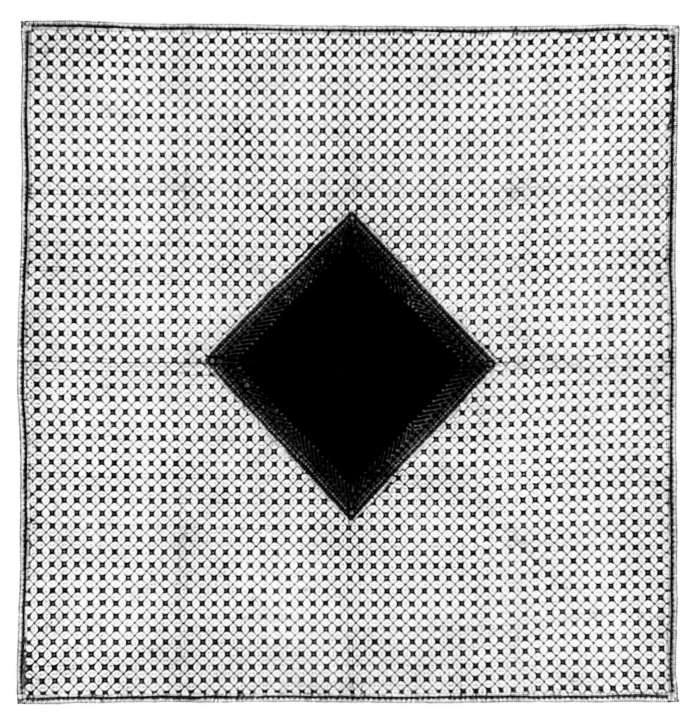

The *kawung* motif which fills the
main field of this headcloth is one
of the designs whose use was
restricted at one time to members
of the royal household in the
Mataram court of Central Java. It is
said by some to represent the fruit
of the sugar palm tree.
Tulis, cotton. 105.5 x 105.5 cm.
(Smend collection)

Combinations of diagonal lines in
which a variety of fine patterns
are juxtaposed are known as
'*udan liris*', or drizzling rain. In
this *kain panjang* from Yogyakarta
the diagonal lines run from top
right to bottom left. *Tulis*, cotton.
106 x 231 cm. (Smend collection)

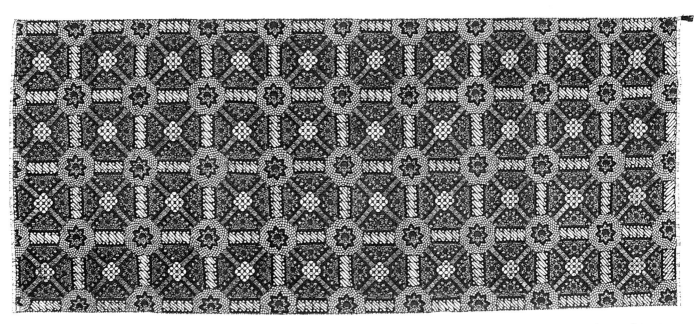

The name of this motif, *ksatrian*,
is a reference to one of the higher
classes of Javanese society. *Kain
panjang. Tulis,* cotton. Yogyakarta.
105 x 245 cm. (Smend collection)

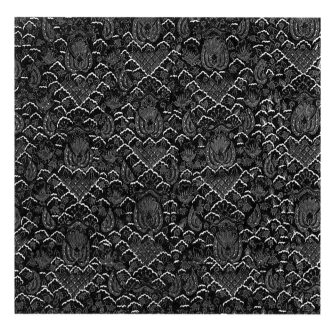

Batik of the court of Surakarta is characterized by a rich brown colour and a deep blue ground. The name of the design, *Semeru*, refers to a holy mountain in the east of Java, once revered as the home of the gods. The mountain peaks are indicated in white, while the throne motif and Garuda are also clearly depicted here. *Tulis*, cotton. 107 x 230 cm. (Smend collection)

The *parang rusak* design is widely associated with Sultan Agung, the 17th-century ruler of the court of Mataram. It is seen as symbolic of royal power and cosmic energy. *Parang Rusak Barong*, the giant-sized version of the motif, was reserved for the use of the ruler himself. *Tulis*, cotton. Surakarta. 107 x 257 cm. (Smend collection)

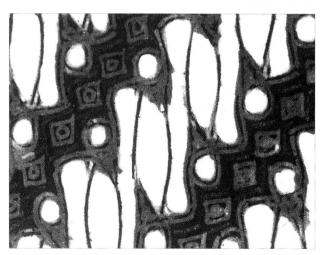

Young noblemen from Solo and Yogyakarta, some of whom are wearing *parang rusak* designs. Fourth from the left is Raden Ario Djajanagoro. To his left is Suryabrongta, brother of Hamengkubuwono IX, and uncle of the present Sultan. Photographer unkown, 1934. (Leo Haks photo collection, Amsterdam)

Although animals do appear in
Javanese batik, the Muslim
prohibition of the depiction of
animals sometimes results in
extreme stylization. The mythical
creature on this cloth is barely
visible. *Tulis*, cotton. Cirebon.
105 x 234.5 cm. (Smend collection)

Detail of a *kain panjang* decorated with the *megamendung* (cloud) motif. *Tulis*, cotton. Gunung Jati workshop, Trusmi, Cirebon, 1995. 104 x 240 cm. (Kerlogue collection)

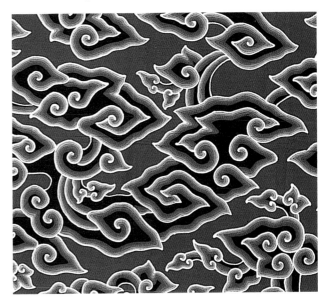

The densely packed dots found in older-style batiks from Tuban (East Java), Indramayu and Cirebon (West Java) are achieved by pricking holes in the waxed surface of the cloth to allow penetration of the dye. This detail is taken from a *kain panjang*. *Tulis*, cotton. Cirebon, ca. 1950. 106 x 245 cm. (Smend collection)

There appears to be a variant of the diagonal *parang* design in the body of this *sarung* from Indramayu, though it is sometimes referred to locally as 'fish hooks'. It may have derived from a court design or the court design may have originally derived from a country motif and been assigned a new meaning in the court context. Similarly, the phoenix and the fan-shaped lotus in the *papan* may have been copied for their decorative shapes rather than their original meanings. *Tulis*, cotton. Indramayu. 110 x 205 cm. (Kerlogue collection)

OPPOSITE: The colour range of the batiks of Indramayu is generally restricted to a dark blue or maroon set against a creamy ground. The replacement of large triangular motifs with smaller ones at one end of the *kain* is also typical. *Tulis*, cotton. Indramayu, 1994. 103 x 242 cm. (Kerlogue collection)

An unusual design from Indramayu has a plain blue central field with patterned borders. Its name, '*kluwungan*', meaning 'angel', relates to the story of a spirit whose clothes were stolen while she was bathing. *Tulis*, cotton. 1994. 106 x 224 cm. (Kerlogue collection)

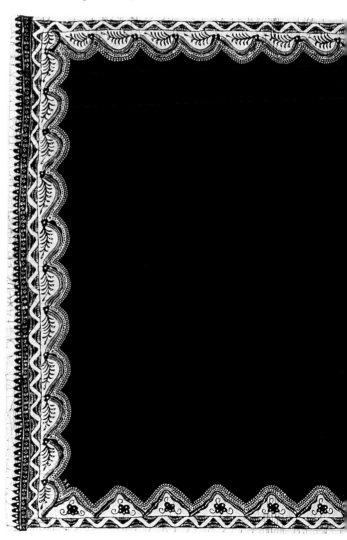

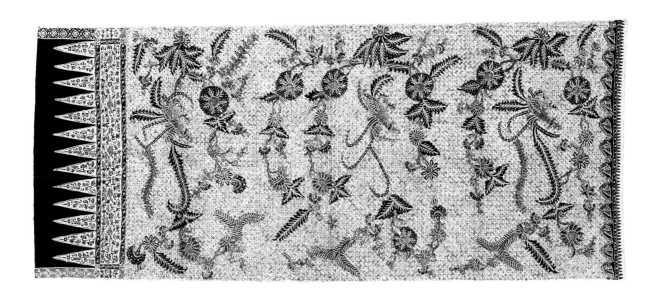

RIGHT: In Pekalongan, the workshops established by Indo-European women in the late 19th and early 20th centuries produced designs which suited the taste of European customers. The fish-scale filling design in the main field is traditionally Javanese, however. *Sarung. Tulis*, cotton. 112 x 106 cm. (Smend collection)

BELOW: Many of the batik makers from Pekalongan are of Chinese origin, and their taste is reflected in the pastel colours of much of their work. This *sarung* is signed Oey Soe Tjoen, Kedungwuni. *Tulis*, cotton. Kedungwuni, ca. 1935. 108 x 209.5 cm. (Smend collection)

BELOW: This detail of a *kain* from Pekalongan shows a combination of the *parang* motif, associated in the past with the courts of Central Java, with a floral design and pastel colour scheme more typical of the north coast. *Tulis*, cotton. Pekalongan. 106 x 260 cm. (Smend collection)

RIGHT: Batik producers in Pekalongan of Arab descent became especially attached to the *jelamprang* design which also evokes the patterns of ceramic tiles in the mosques of the Middle East. The unusual dark green, the colour of Islam, is also a favourite amongst Arab makers and customers. *Tulis*, cotton. 107 x 250 cm. (Smend collection)

BELOW: Batik producers of Dutch descent in Pekalongan often drew their inspiration from illustrations in European books. Children's fairy tales were a popular subject, as in this delightful *sarung* from the workshop of Mrs. Metzelaar, depicting scenes from *The Sleeping Beauty*. *Tulis*, cotton. Pekalongan, ca. 1910. 108 x 250 cm. (Smend collection)

OPPOSITE TOP: Batik produced in Pekalongan for clients of Chinese descent was often dyed in soft pastel colours similar to those found in the imported ceramics popular amongst the Chinese community. This design is *cempaka warna*, or coloured *kamboja* flowers. *Sarung. Tulis*, cotton, chemical dyes. Signed Tan Kok Hwi. 107 x 205 cm. (Smend collection)

OPPOSITE BOTTOM: On the north coast, the two ends of skirt cloths were often separated with a diagonal division. This kind of cloth was known as a *kain pagi-sore* (morning-afternoon) since the wearer could choose which side of the design to expose according to the time of day or the occasion. The irises in blue and pale apricot repeated in each half ensure continuity between the two halves. This example is from the workshop of Oey Soe Tjoen, who together with his wife produced exceptionally fine batik in Kedungwuni from the 1920s until 1976, when their children took over both the workshop and signature. *Tulis*, cotton. 106 x 258 cm. (Smend collection)

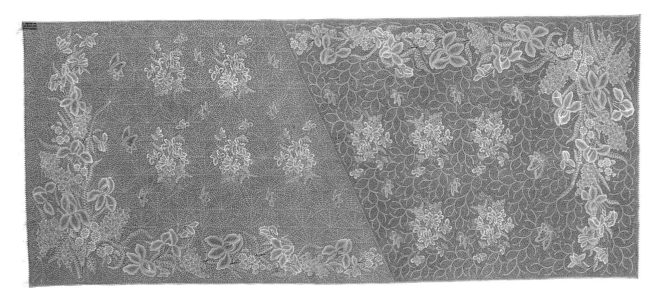

BELOW: This lively ceremonial cloth, or *mui li*, has all the hallmarks of Lasem, from the strong clear red on a cream ground to the delicately drawn animal motifs. There are also representations of some of the eight Buddhist treasures, auspicious symbols characteristic of textiles made by and for the Chinese community. *Tulis*, cotton. Lasem, late 19th to early 20th century. 92 x 201 cm. (Smend collection)

OPPOSITE: *Batik tiga negeri*, 'three-country batik', was produced through a system that involved three batik centres. In a typical piece, the cloth might be waxed and dyed first in Lasem, where the rich Turkey-red colour was applied. After that it might go to Pekalongan for the second waxing and a second dyebath before finally being sent to Surakarta, where it was finished in *soga* brown. The designs were often a combination of Central Javanese court motifs and coastal elements. *Tulis*, cotton. Signed Nj. T. T. Ting, Solo. Lasem, Pekalongan and Surakarta, first half of the 20th century. 105 x 204 cm. (Smend collection)

BELOW: The red and cream colour
scheme for which Lasem was
once famous is referred to in Java
as *bang-bangan*. For weddings,
elaborately decorated bedspreads
(*kain sprei*) were made.
Tulis, cotton. 208 x 288 cm.
(Smend collection)

OPPOSITE TOP: Stamford Raffles
commented in the early 19th
century on the red dyes used by
Malays on the north coast of Java.
This *kain panjang* was probably
made for export to Sumatra.
Tulis, cotton, natural dyes. Lasem,
late 19th to early 20th century.
108 x 252 cm. (Kerlogue collection)

OPPOSITE BOTTOM: The edges of this
batik were waxed and dyed in
Lasem before it was sold on as a
kain blangko, or blank cloth. The
central area was then waxed and
dyed at a workshop in a different
town. *Tulis*, cotton. Lasem and
Pekalongan, late 19th to early
20th century. 105 x 254 cm.
(Smend collection)

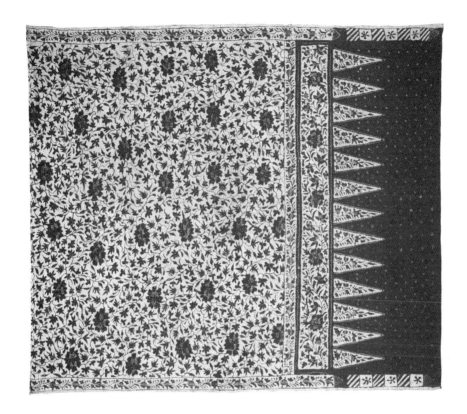

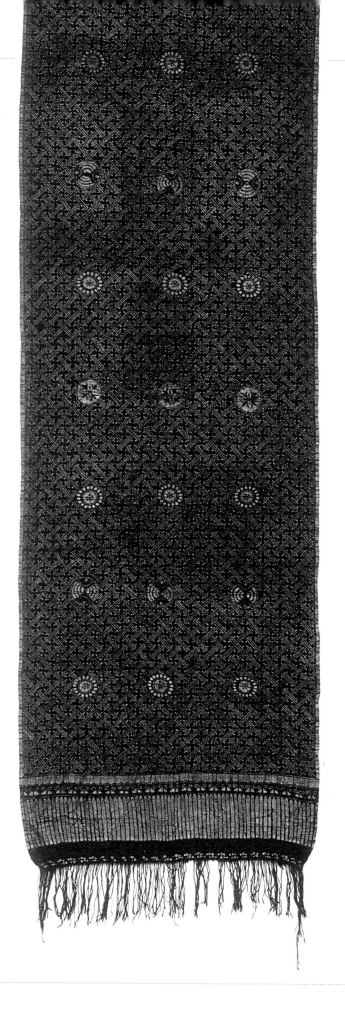

RIGHT: *Putihan*, a ritual cloth from the Tuban area. It is known as *panji lori* or *panji serong* and is displayed on ritual occasions. Its geometric motifs distinguish it from everyday *putihan* cloth, which is decorated with floral and vegetal motifs. *Tulis*, homespun handwoven cotton. Tuban. 88 x 264 cm. (Inv. no. 109727, Museon, The Hague)

OPPOSITE: *Sayut bangrod*. Unmarried girls in the Tuban area wear the *bangrod*, characterized by red designs of seedlings, flowers and birds on a white ground. *Selendang*. *Tulis*, homespun handwoven cotton. Tuban. 56 x 320 cm. (Inv. no. 109708, Museon, The Hague)

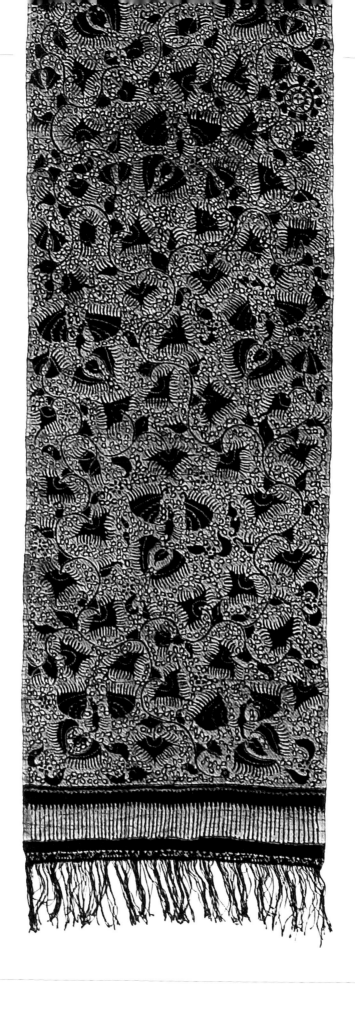

OPPOSITE: *Pipitan*, a shoulder cloth
coloured in red, blue and black,
which is worn in the Tuban area
by the middle generation of
married women with children.
Tulis, homespun handwoven
cotton. Margorejo, Tuban, 1990s.
58 x 328 cm. (Kerlogue collection)

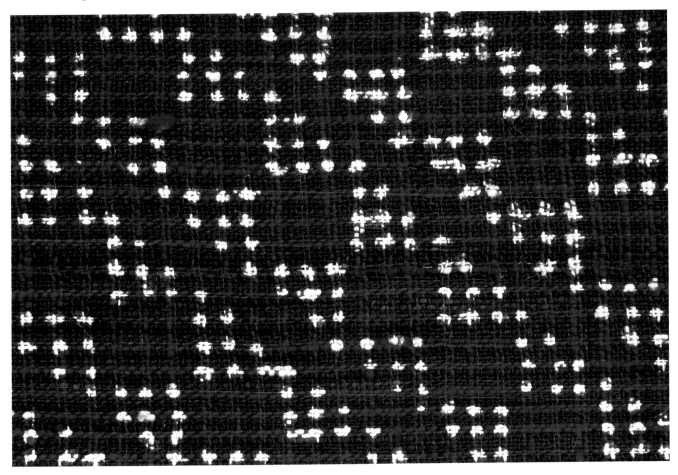

(DETAIL OF PAGE 23 TOP) *Batik lurik* is
produced by applying dots of wax
to a cloth woven in a blue and
white striped or chequered
design. The cloth is then immersed
in a red dyebath. When the wax
is removed, the result is a cloth of
three colours with a white dotted
design. This pattern is named
kijing miring, which means 'slanting
tombstones'. *Tulis*, handwoven
homespun cotton. Margorejo,
Tuban, 1990s. 51 x 200 cm.
(Kerlogue collection)

ABOVE: Silk scarves were made in the area between Rembang, Juana and Pati, often for export to Bali and West Sumatra. The designs show much evidence of Chinese influence, particularly in the depictions of the stylized phoenixes and the fretwork border. They were usually dyed in blue or brown, with the background echoing the main colour in a paler tone. The finished product was known as *lokcan*, literally 'blue silk'. This example was collected in Klungkung, Bali. *Tulis*, silk. Juana/Rembang/Pati, early 20th century. 48 x 190 cm. (Smend collection)

OPPOSITE BOTTOM: The lines which protrude from the motifs on this *lokcan sarung* are called *ren* (thorn), and are typical of the style of the eastern Pasisir. The *kepala* is broken up into the *gigi balang* form, with smaller triangles beneath the main *pucuk rebung* triangles on either side of a thickly outlined vertical row of diamonds. The pairs of birds of paradise which dominate the *sarung* and the large floral motifs into which they are set are boldly drawn; the skirt was exported to Bali where it would have been worn by a dancer and where fineness of detail would not have been required. *Tulis*, silk. Juana/Rembang/Pati, collected in Bali, early 20th century. 99.5 x 160 cm. (Smend collection)

ABOVE: In West Sumatra squares of *lokcan* imported from Java were used to cover areca nut containers used in ceremonies. Others were used as handkerchiefs for Peranakan brides. *Tulis*, silk. 54.5 x 54 cm. (Smend collection)

OPPOSITE TOP: Many women in coastal Madura supplement their income by making batik while their husbands are away at sea or working overseas, and motifs often relate to the maritime environment. The bands in the background of this *sarung* are referred to as *Tase Malaya*, or Malayan Sea, and are typically filled with a variety of filling motifs, or *guri*. *Tulis*, cotton. Tanjung Bumi, Madura, recent. 112 x 196 cm. (Willach collection)

OPPOSITE BOTTOM: Like Lasem, Madura is famous for its vibrant red dye. As in Java, the main ingredient was the root of the *mengkudu* tree, but both the other ingredients and the processes differed from those employed in Javanese versions. In Madura, *kain panjang* like this are known as *samper*. The filling design is *ramuk* (roots). *Tulis*, cotton. Tanjung Bumi, Madura, 1998. 104 x 248 cm. (Kerlogue collection)

ABOVE: *Si Basi* (bowls). Set against the background of *sesse* (scales) are the shapes of swifts (*burung dedeli*). *Tulis*, cotton. Putri Madura workshop, Telaga Biru, Madura, 1998. 105 x 190 cm. (Tropenmuseum, Amsterdam)

(DETAIL OF PAGE 59 TOP) Four different *guri* (filling motifs) appear in the circles which give the design of this *sarung* its name: *carcena, kembang kopi, korek tikar* and *testes*.

BELOW: In Madura, batik is made
to suit all pockets, and simpler
designs like this one make
inexpensive batik garments
available to everyone. Batik is still
worn widely by men, women
and children, especially in the
Bangkalan region. *Tulis*, cotton.
1993. 105 x 210 cm.
(Kerlogue collection)

OPPOSITE: A frequent feature of
the batik of Madura is the
appearance of the *burung suari*,
the peacock, or 'bird with a
voice'. The treatment of the
bird's plumage and the
background motifs by dividing
them into balanced patches of
colour is also typically Madurese.
Sarung. Tulis, cotton. 1960s.
105 x 188 cm.
(Kerlogue collection)

At first sight the design of this batik, known as '*Merak Ngeram*' or 'brooding peahen', appears to have been printed on, with its repeating shapes regularly spaced across the cloth. In fact it has been meticulously drawn by hand. The art of dyeing with red was a closely guarded secret in Jambi, so that for a long time it was believed by many that no red was used there and that these fine cloths were imported. *Tulis*, cotton. 92.5 x 218.5 cm. (Smend collection)

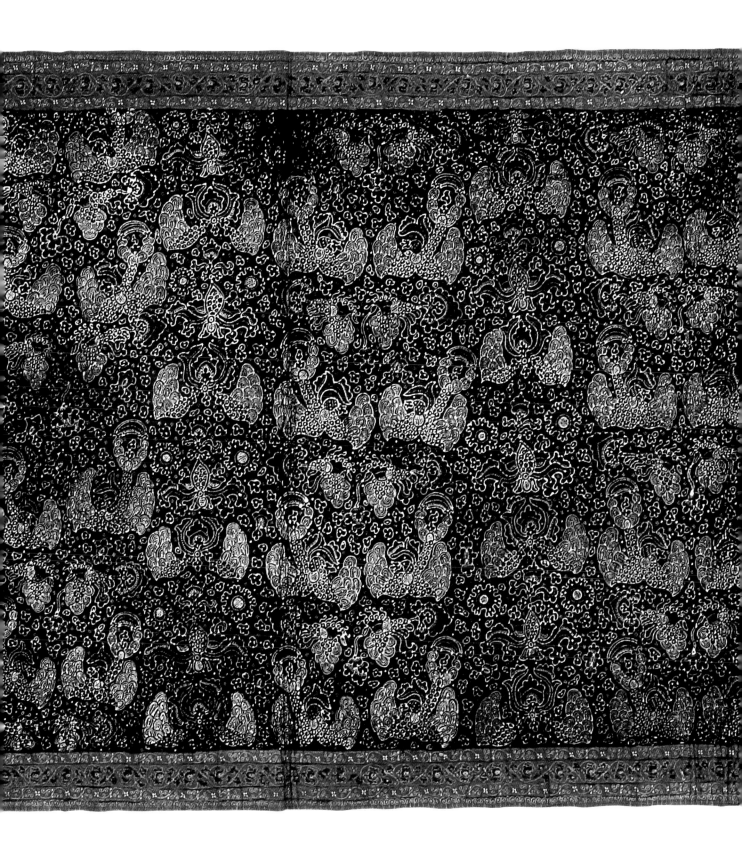

OPPOSITE: An unusual type of batik still being made in Jambi differs on each face of the cloth. Forerunners of these cloths, which are known as *siang-malam* (day-night), were used to cover the bier at burials. They are no longer used for this purpose, and their rich colours and unique effect make them highly prized pieces. *Tulis*, cotton. Batik Asmah workshop, Olak Kemang, Jambi, 1990s. 104 x 222 cm. (Kerloque collection)

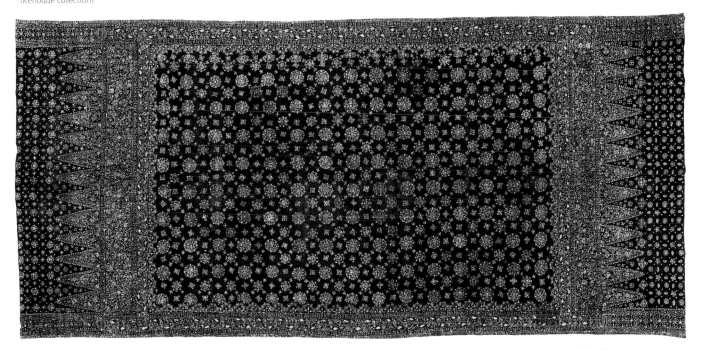

ABOVE: When Dutch commentators first came across batik in Jambi in the 1920s they were struck by the effect of gold created by allowing an overdye of ruddy *marelang* to seep into cracks in the wax covering the areas dyed yellow with *lembato*. The effect is clearly visible in this *kain panjang*, decorated with the *kaca piring* (gardenia) design. *Tulis*, cotton. Late 19th to early 20th century. 105.5 x 250.5 cm. (Smend collection)

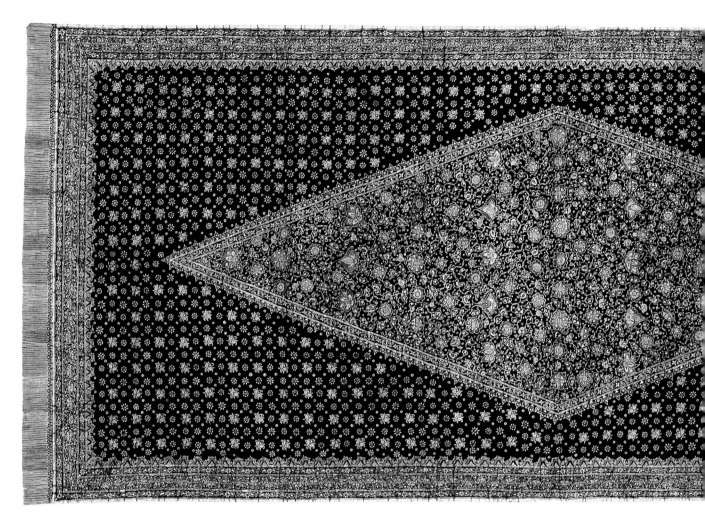

In Jambi, *selendang* with a central lozenge are known as *selendang bersidang*. The combination of regular rows of half-drops in the main field with a central lozenge filled with tendrils and leaves is typical, as is the triple border. *Tulis*, cotton. Early 20th century. 91 x 209.5 cm. (Smend collection)

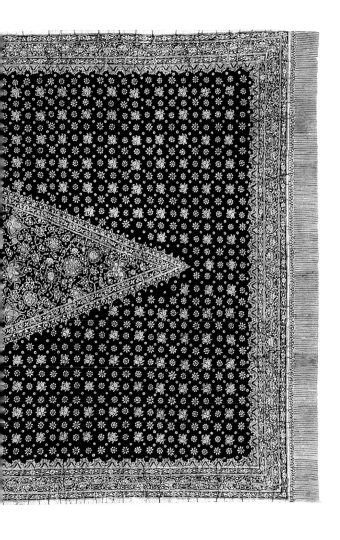

Cloths known as *batik bersurat* were covered in Arabic script and other designs which reflect those found in Middle Eastern contexts. They may have been copied from textiles brought back by pilgrims from Mecca. Many are found in Sumatra, where they were once used as headcloths or to cover the bier of a devout Muslim. Red signifies bravery and this cloth may have been used to cover a fallen fighter in the struggle for independence.
Tulis, heavy cotton cloth.
94 x 218 cm. (Smend collection)

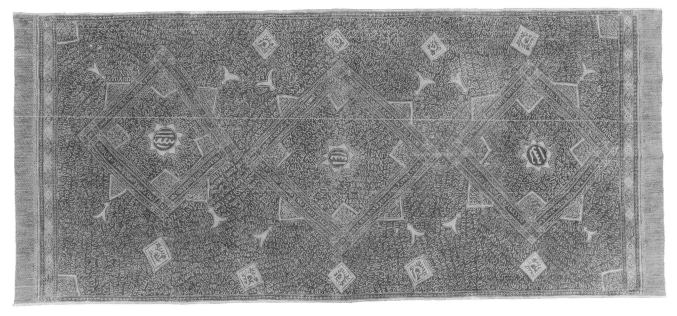

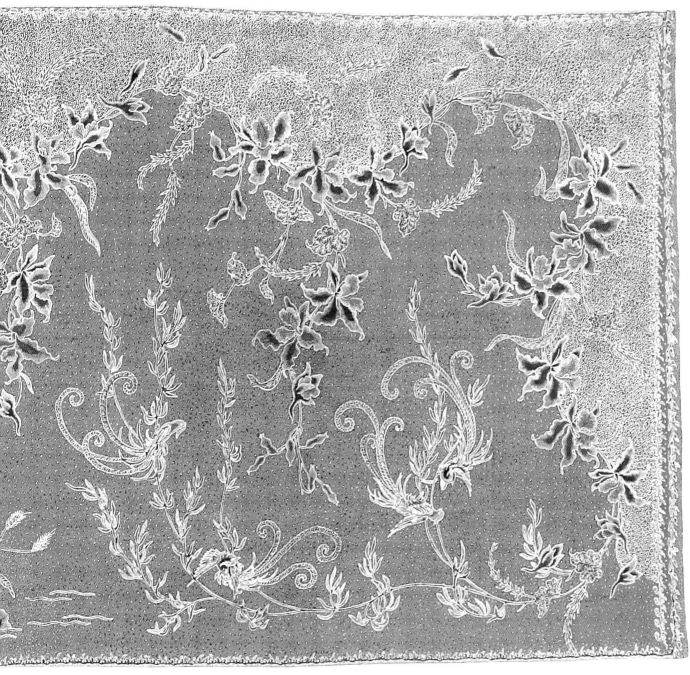

Entrepreneurs of Chinese descent in Demak and Kudus were known for their very fine batik. Backgrounds of cloths from these centres are typically very intricately patterned in a warm *soga* brown. The wide border panel in the top right is known as *terang bulan*.
Kain panjang. Tulis, cotton. Signed Liem Siok Hien, Kudus. 107.5 x 261.5 cm. (Smend collection)

One famous enterprise was run
by the Arab Al Juffri family,
whose batik was very popular in
Sumatra. They specialized in the
khudung, a kind of *selendang*
large enough to cover a woman's
head and shoulders. Headcloths
of this size are widely worn
amongst the Muslim community
in eastern Sumatra, though styles
have changed. *Tulis*, cotton.
Late 19th century. 91 x 200 cm.
(Smend collection)

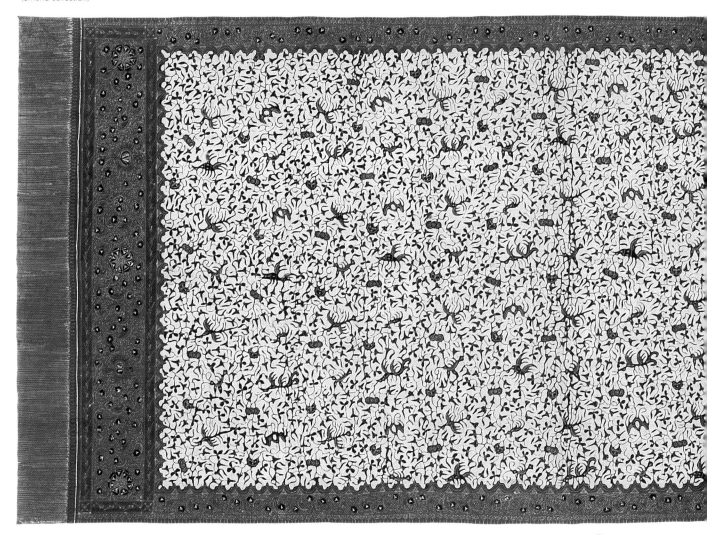

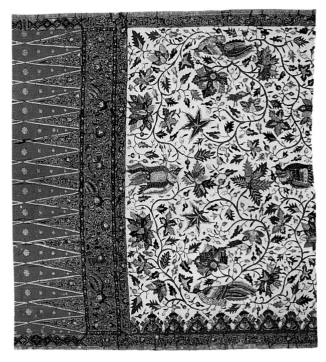

When only small areas of colour are required in particular parts of the cloth, the dye can sometimes be painted on. This process is usually referred to as *coletan*, and the blue areas of this cloth have been applied in this way. The red dye, in this case a mixture of *mengkudu* and the mordant *jirak*, has been brushed onto the cloth in a process known as *dulitan*, peculiar to East Java and parts of Madura. *Tulis*, *colet* and *dulit*, cotton. Gresik, early 20th century. 106 x 198 cm. (Kerlogue collection)

FOLLOWING PAGES: Scenes from *wayang kulit* shadow theatre performances are replicated in this traditional design depicting a contest between *ksatria*, or members of the warrior class. To the left of centre in the second row the huge figure of Sena (or Bima) can be seen with his four brothers. At the top, three of the *punakawan*, companions of the Pendawa brothers, with odd-shaped noses and pot bellies, also appear. *Wayang Cirebon*. *Tulis*, cotton. Ibu Masina, Trusmi, Cirebon, 1970s. 106 x 244 cm. (Smend collection)

3

Motifs and Meanings

Batik is one of the most meaningful forms of art in Indonesia, so that the cloths have come to be seen as symbolic of many of the values held most dear by the culture which produces them. They are used in ritual contexts, at name-giving ceremonies for babies, at circumcisions, at weddings and at royal investitures. Their meanings are partly associated with the way the batik cloths are used: how they are folded, where they are placed and to whom they are given. In addition, many of the motifs carry meaning, but these are many and varied. One motif may mean different things to different people, and the name of a pattern will vary from one region to another. Even within one village the name and significance of a motif may differ from one household or workshop to the next. The name of a motif may act as a label describing the shape, and may bear no relation to its meaning. On the other hand, some motif names do encapsulate the significance accorded to the design. Many of these motifs have acquired a more wide-spread significance, such that there is general agreement about what they mean.

OPPOSITE: The double wings and tail feathers of Garuda, combined in the aristocratic *sawat* motif, are prominent here. Garuda is the vehicle on which the Hindu god Vishnu travels, but the wing motif has wider connotations today. To many it is suggestive of the wings of the Bouraq, which carried Mohammed to heaven. *Kain panjang. Tulis*, cotton. Central Java. 108 x 230 cm. (Smend collection)

Javanese motifs

Many Javanese people have no knowledge of the significance of batik patterns; those who do will interpret them in different ways, and will probably refer to a pattern's character rather than its meaning. Objects represented in a pattern may themselves be acting as symbols; the way in which the object is stylized may also convey some meaning. Thus a butterfly motif might attempt to convey the flitting, fleeting airy aspect of a butterfly's flight and may bear little resemblance to a butterfly as seen in life.

Some motifs convey moral messages. The pattern known as '*kopi pecah*' (broken coffee beans) is sometimes said to contain the lesson that one should be willing to sacrifice oneself to serve the common interest. The *kawung* motif has been said to symbolize the hope that the wearer will be as useful to the community as the *kawung* palm. The filling design *ukel*, on the other hand, derives a meaning from the dance movement which bears the same name and which resembles the hand movement of the batik artist as she draws the design on the cloth.

While all batik motifs have associations and meanings for some people, it is the designs of the Central Javanese palaces, or *kraton*, which are the most well documented. One set of *larangan* (proscribed) designs contained some of the *semen* patterns, consisting of young shoots of foliage; those containing the *mirong* motif (single or double wings) or the *sawat* motif (double wings with outspread tail feathers) were reserved for princes and their wives, and sons and daughters of the king. *Semen* designs without *sawat* motifs, *kawung* designs and the cursive slanting motif known as *rujak sente*

were the dress of the upper level of the aristocracy known as *raden mas* and *raden*. The meanings of such designs are said to be related to Hindu–Javanese philosophy. The wings of the *mirong* and *sawat* motifs are associated with Garuda, the bird-man vehicle of Vishnu, the preserver and destroyer.

Another set of proscribed designs, those in the *parang rusak* group, are thought by some scholars to derive from the North Sumatran motif named '*padang rusa*', (deer pasture). However, a legend tells how Prince Panji, a fabled prince of Java, was once saved by the protective power of the *parang rusak* motif, while another recounts how the first Muslim ruler of Mataram, Sultan Agung, created the design after contemplating a stretch of jagged rocks on the south coast. Both the shape of the motif and its significance have undergone changes over the centuries, and although those attending court ceremonies still respect the ancient prohibitions, few Indonesians today are aware of the original significance ascribed to these motifs.

In addition to the *larangan* motifs restricted to royal use, there are countless others which have meanings making them suitable for wearing on particular occasions: the *sido asih* expresses a wish for everlasting love, while the *sido mukti* expresses a wish for prosperity. These *sido* motifs are characterized by a lattice pattern enclosing motifs which depict items symbolizing what is wished for: a house (symbolizing shelter), a butterfly (fertility and the continuation of the family line), a wing (aspiration) or a flower (fragrance). Batik cloths with *sido* motifs are often worn by the bride and groom on the occasion of their wedding. The parents at a Central Javanese wedding ceremony commonly wear a motif known

Batik designs from Central Java documented by Pirngadie in the early 20th century. FAR LEFT: *Kawung Picisan*. LEFT: *Kawung Beton*. (Jasper and Pirngadie, figs. 202 and 201)
More batik designs recorded by Pirngadie. RIGHT: *Ayam Puger*. FAR RIGHT: *Parang Baris*. (Jasper and Pirngadie, figs. 154 and 207)

as 'truntum'. Some say that this means 'budding', while others say it means 'to guide' or to 'lead'.

At the Cirebon *kraton*, one of the oldest groups of designs is the *taman arum*, or perfumed garden. The name refers to the abode of the gods but also to the royal garden, where the sultan would go to meditate and achieve a state of spiritual detachment from the material world. The batik design depicts the rocks, trees and flowers in the garden in a flat, two-dimensional form. At the same time it shows the stages in life through which a man must go to achieve a transcendant state, with clear echoes of the life of the Buddha. First there is the mundane everyday world, represented by animals such as the deer and the wild boar, symbolizing strength. In the second stage there is often a banyan tree, interpreted today as representing age and wisdom, though the parallel with the forest in which the Buddha sought enlightenment is clear. Later stages depict a fish in a pond, representing good luck and fertility, and a pavilion, representing the centre of the earth and the base on which all is founded. Finally, phoenixes are depicted, symbolizing reincarnation.

Chinese iconography

In centres such as Pekalongan and Lasem, much of the batik production is still in the hands of entrepreneurs of Chinese ethnic origin. In the past, traditional culture remained strong in the Chinese communities, and motifs with clear symbolic meanings were incorporated into the batik. For Chinese customers, these motifs carried unambiguous significance. For others, the meanings were often read in different ways. What were once Chinese symbols became incorporated into batik made for the Javanese market.

The swastika motif has ancient origins in both India and China, but the name by which it is widely known in Indonesia, '*banji*', derives from the Chinese words '*ban*' and '*zi*' meaning 'ten' and 'thousand'. To the Chinese the motif thus has connotations of infinity and hence immortality, but it is also widely used in Javanese and Madurese batik, usually as a filler design.

One of the most persistent images is the flying phoenix, which traditionally represented both rebirth and the female *yin* principle. In imperial China this image was associated with the empress, and as a bride was deemed to be 'empress for the day', this was often the motif which appeared on a bride's skirt cloth. The dragon represented the emperor, but two opposing dragons expressed perfection. The double dragon motif is now customarily used on *gendongan* cloths, in which babies are carried in all the north coast regions of Java by mothers from all ethnic groups.

In Chinese folk art, signs and symbols often have double meanings. For example, the Chinese character for fish also means abundance, so the image of a fish would carry this connotation too. Another image which commonly appears in batik from Java, especially from the north coast, is the *qilin*, which is shaped like a lion but has fish scales, hooves and sometimes a horn. In Confucianism the *qilin* is associated with felicity and longevity. Nowadays few are aware of such meanings, but the motifs continue to be used, having acquired more general connotations of auspiciousness and good fortune among the community at large.

Malay meanings

Among the Malay population of Jambi, the names and meanings ascribed to batik motifs differ from those found in Java. In Malay textiles, the designs consist in the main of patterns of fruit and flowers, often repeated in symmetrical rows across the cloth. The flowers depicted are usually the ones used at weddings and name-giving ceremonies to lend their sweet perfume to the occasion, gardenia and jasmine being the favourites. Cucumber seeds and the mangosteen calyx are often included in the design, probably because of their association with fertility. The *duren pecah* is a popular motif which Dutch scholars in the last century assumed to have been derived from the Javanese *mirong*. If it was indeed copied from a Javanese design, it nevertheless carried a quite different meaning, being interpreted locally as a split durian fruit, of central importance in Jambi culture.

A characteristic design in Jambi is the *selendang bersidang*, a headcloth worn by women with an elongated lozenge in the centrefield. These cloths may once have been associated with the court of the Jambi sultan. Today they are worn by mature women outside the house to protect them from the sun. Of the more complex designs, *Batanghari* is a variant of the 'tree of life' motif, which links heaven and earth. This particular style may have been drawn from that of Indian imported *palempore* cloths, though its resonance would result from the significance which the tree motif already carried in Indonesia. Another popular motif in Jambi is the *Kapal Sanggat*, or stranded ship. Although motifs with similar names appear elsewhere, their appearance differs markedly, and this design seems to be peculiar to Jambi. The meaning may relate to the shallow waters of the river, whose basin delineates the boundaries of the Jambi area and where visiting merchants were often stranded on their way to the harbour. This motif has come to be seen as particularly expressive of local identity.

Colour

Batik cloths are often referred to in relation to their main colours, especially of the background. *Latar ireng* is a cloth with a white background; *bang-bangan* refers to a cloth characterized by a dominant red. Some cloths acquire a special significance resulting from a combination of colours. Red, associated with the female principle, and white, associated with the male principle, in combination represent fertility and prosperity. At marriage ceremonies in parts of Java, the bride and groom are draped with a red-and-white cloth to unite them and to confer these qualities on their union.

Green and white together can be interpreted as the green leaves and white flower of the jasmine. This is the flower of Nyi Roro Kidul, the legendary Queen of the South Seas to whom the rulers of Mataram were symbolically wedded. Cloths in this colour combination are offered to her at the annual Labuhan ceremony held in her honour by the Sultan of Yogyakarta. Legend has it that she will capture any man wearing green who walks on the south Javanese shore.

The colours of batik cloths sometimes have a significance which relates to the stage in the life cycle of the wearer. In Kerek, in northeastern Java, there seems to be a system at work in which the colours appropriate for a particular wearer or a particular occasion may relate to cosmological classifications. The Javanese associate the four main colour categories of white, red, yellow and blue-black with the four cardinal points. White is associated with the east, origins and birth; red with south and fertility; yellow with the west and maturity; and blue-black with the north and death. The actual visible colours of the cloths worn at life cycle rituals do not always reflect this pattern, but the underlying dyes used do seem to correspond to it.

Calligraphy

The production of batik with Islamic calligraphy has experienced a recent revival. In the nineteenth and early twentieth centuries many of these cloths were used in Sumatra, worn as headcloths by lineage chiefs in the Padang highlands or by fighters in the struggle for independence to protect themselves against bullets from enemy guns. The motifs on these cloths had particular meanings, some overt but others mystical and deeply symbolic.

Phrases from the Qur'an which appear most commonly are the *shahadah*, the Muslim profession of faith, or the *basmallah*, a phrase used at the start of each of the suras of the Qur'an and also uttered before any major undertaking. Another common feature is the Dhu'l-Faqar, the double-bladed sword of Ali, son-in-law of the prophet Mohammed. The star-shaped Seal of Solomon also appears frequently, with either five points made from one continuous line, or six points made from two triangles, one superimposed on the other. Some calligraphic phrases are arranged into the shapes of birds or lions, both of which carry religious significance.

In many motifs the meanings are encoded, with numbers often representing letters, or vice versa, in a cabbalistic arrangement. This is particularly prevalent in the cloths sewn into talismanic shirts. There are records of Turkish soldiers wearing this type of shirt into battle and the practice in Indonesia may have resulted from links with the Ottomans. One particular motif which expresses connections with Turkey is the *tughra*, the emblematic signature of the Ottoman sultans. This is a common design component in the square headcloths. Although the precise meaning of some of the elements in these calligraphy batiks may remain shrouded in mystery, their role as an expression of devotion to the faith is unquestionable.

Many traditional Cirebon designs are composed of elements reflecting syncretism in religious beliefs and cultural ideas. On this *kain panjang* the Chinese *qilin*, a symbol of long life and happiness, appears in combination with the wings of the Hindu Garuda. The colour scheme is unusual, but appropriate as green is the colour of Islam. *Tulis*, cotton. 1975. 106 x 245 cm. (Smend collection)

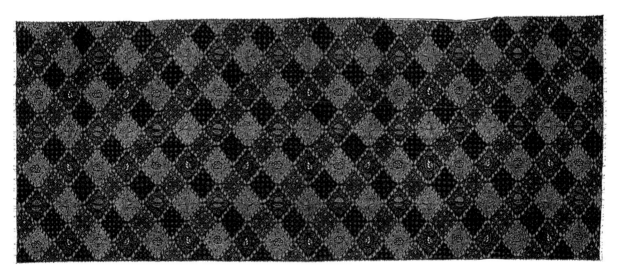

This *kain* is decorated with a version of the *sido wirasat* design, meaning 'a wish to give advice'. It is made up of a lattice in between which appear auspicious images, including the star-like *truntum* motif, a reference to budding love. The design may be worn by the parents of a bride to express their willingness to give guidance to the couple. *Tulis*, cotton. Yogyakarta. 105.5 x 232 cm. (Smend collection)

Sekar jagad (literally 'flowers of the universe') is worn as part of the Central Javanese marriage ceremony. It is said to express the heartfelt joy felt by a girl or boy at having found their partner. *Kain panjang. Tulis*, cotton. Surakarta. 106 x 266.5 cm. (Smend collection)

The *naga*, or serpent, is an old
Hindu-Javanese emblem, symbolic
of the watery realm. It is usually
depicted with a crown, as is this
one. The *naga* is a powerful
supernatural creature, but is
usually benign and is generally
regarded in Java as a protective
presence. *Kain panjang.*
Tulis, cotton. Central Java.
106.5 x 232 cm. (Smend collection)

Patchwork garments were
sometimes worn by Buddhist
priests in old Java as part of their
vow of poverty, and a patchwork
jacket belonging to the sultans of
Yogyakarta was believed to have
great protective power. It is
possible that such concepts
underlie the development of the
tambal batik design. *Tulis*, cotton.
Yogyakarta, ca. 1940.
105 x 250 cm. (Smend collection)

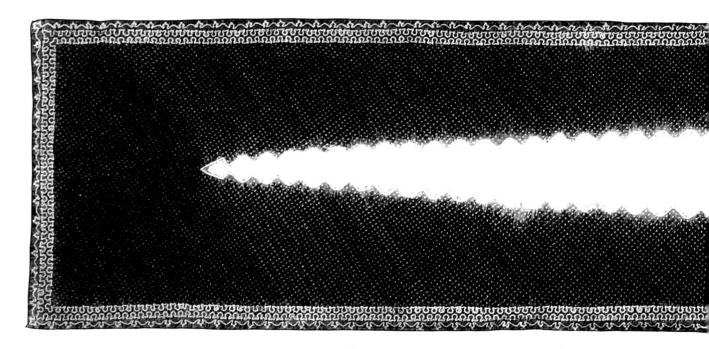

The design on this *kemben* has been produced by a variant of batik known as *tritik*, in which the dye is resisted by sewn or tied elements. The central lozenge, *sidhangan*, is a female symbol and is traditionally worn only by married women. *Tritik*, cotton. Central Java, first half of the 20th century. 52.5 x 253 cm. (Smend collection)

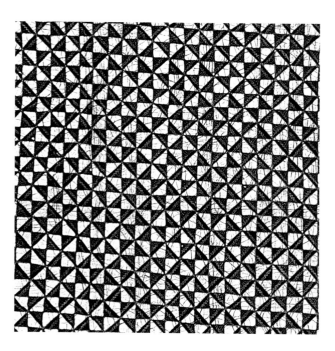

Kain panjang kopi pecah (split coffee beans). A similar motif appears on the painted bark cloths of the Toraja people in Sulawesi. This design is widespread in Central Java and is believed by some to have its origins in a cosmological symbol referring to the cardinal points. *Tulis*, cotton. Central Java. 104.5 x 232.5 cm. (Smend collection)

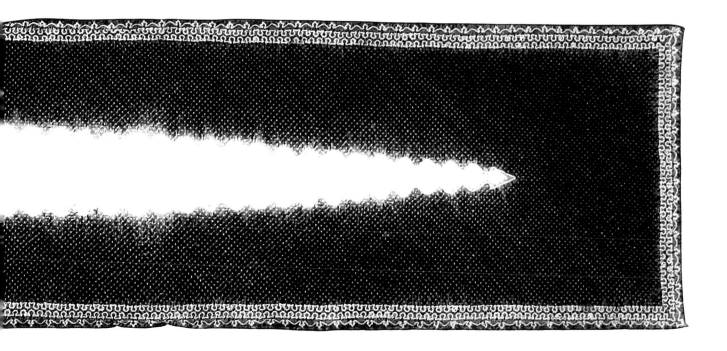

The 'Pisan Bali' design can be
found in the stone carvings of
9th-century Javanese temples and
occurs in batik in many variations.
It symbolizes respect, rank and
social status. *Kain panjang.*
Tulis, cotton. Surakarta.
104 x 231 cm. (Smend collection)

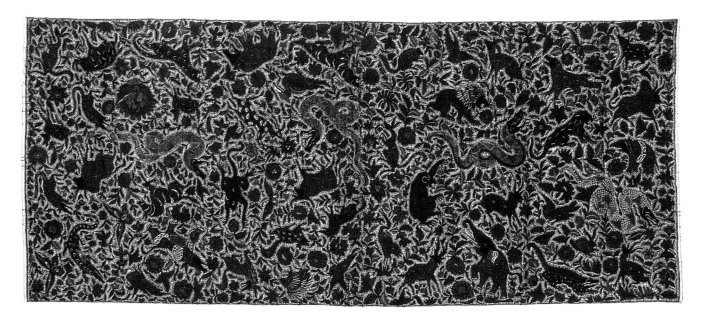

ABOVE: *Kain* decorated with a version of the *alas-alasan* (forest) design. Many of the animals are native species, but some are not: there is a kangaroo and a lion as well as a tapir, probably derived from book illustrations. In *kebun binatang* (zoo) designs, the animals are usually caged. *Tulis*, cotton. Solo, ca. 1975. 106 x 251.5 cm. (Smend collection)

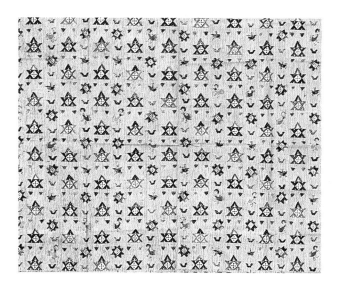

LEFT: *Ayam Puger*, or 'caged rooster', is said to represent the heroism of Prince Puger, who, in approximately 1680, when Mataram was besieged by civil war, was forced to retreat to Banyumas by Dutch-supported Amangkurat II. The motifs are a rooster, a stylized rice barn, a rice mortar, and a directional symbol. *Tulis*, cotton. Banyumas. 108 x 255 cm. (Smend collection)

OPPOSITE: Many batiks from the north coast of Java, the Pasisir, are decorated with designs based on sea creatures. The name of this one, '*ganggeng*', refers to the seaweed strands encircling lobsters, fish, crabs and other sea creatures on the *badan* of this *sarung*. *Tulis*, cotton. 105 x 196 cm. (Smend collection)

RIGHT: The elaborate decorations of this luxurious Indo-European *sarung* are clear indications of its meaning: the extravagant garlands of heart-shaped leaves can only suggest that love has been declared, and the crosses emerging from behind the profusion of flowers in the *kepala* declare that the union is to be sanctioned by the church. Clusters of tiny white jasmine flowers suggest the fragrance of the occasion. *Tulis*, cotton. Ca. 1890–1910. 85 x 140 cm. (Private collection)

OPPOSITE: European symbolism is often evident in skirt cloths made for European and Indo-European customers. This *sarung*, signed E. van Zuylen, contains tiny crosses, anchors and heart-shaped leaves, together signifying faith, hope and charity. The fairly sombre colours suggest that this cloth may have been made for a mature woman. *Tulis*, cotton. First quarter of the 20th century. 105.5 x 90 cm. (Smend collection)

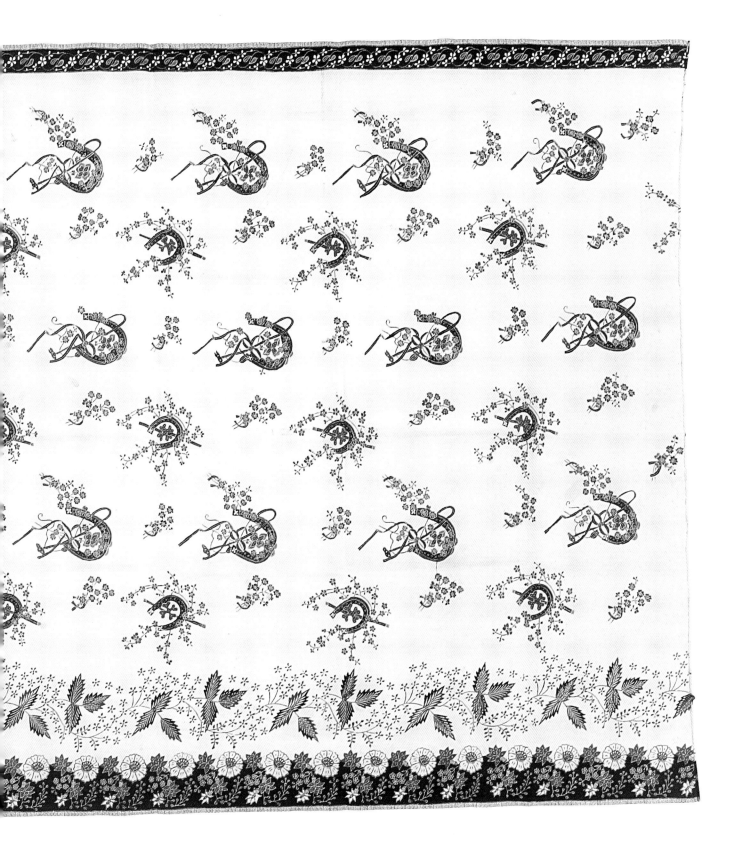

PREVIOUS PAGES: The occasion for which this *sarung* was designed is abundantly clear from the combination of pink ribbons and horseshoes. Although the association of horseshoes with good luck is a European tradition, they also carry this meaning in Indonesia, hence their use on this pretty wedding skirt. *Tulis*, cotton. Pasisir, early 20th century. 108 x 209 cm. (Smend collection)

ABOVE: The designs and script on this ceremonial cloth, produced and used by Chinese Indonesians, are full of symbolic significance. The ideas expressed in the characters, which read from right to left, relate to the importance of expressing respect by performing the appropriate rites for one's ancestors, while the dragon with a pearl beneath its chin is a symbol of male vigour and prosperity. The cloth may have been used at a funeral, or at Qing Ming, the annual festival when the family tombs would be swept. *Tulis*, cotton, chemical dyes. First half of the 20th century. 98 x 103 cm. (Smend collection)

Each of the creatures which are depicted on the *badan* of this *sarung* would have been included for their auspicious significance. The butterflies, which usually refer to wedded bliss, suggest that this was a bridal *sarung*. The bat is a traditional Chinese symbol of longevity. *Tulis*, cotton. Lasem, ca. 1920. 105 x 209 cm. (Smend collection)

This *gendongan*, or carrying
cloth, was probably intended for
use as a baby carrier. The filling
pattern known as '*banji*' was
regarded in Chinese folk
tradition as having talismanic
properties, and of multiplying the
effects of other symbolic motifs
on the cloth. *Tulis*, cotton.
Pekalongan, 1920s.
52.5 x 245 cm.
(Smend collection)

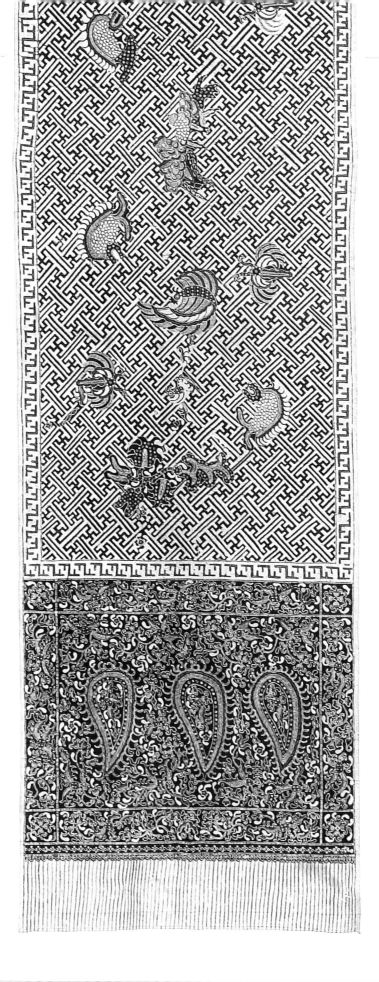

A studio portrait of two Batavia
ladies taken around 1890. The
woman on the right is wearing a
sarung with a *lokcan* design.
Kassian Céphas. (Yu-Chee Chong
Fine Art, London)

This detail from a *kain sprei*, or
bed spread, shows a selection of
typical *lokcan* bird and animal
motifs such as the phoenix, the
lion and the butterfly. The
phoenix was a symbol of the
Chinese Empress, and by
extension the female principle.
Tulis, cotton. 83.5 x 102.5 cm.
(Smend collection)

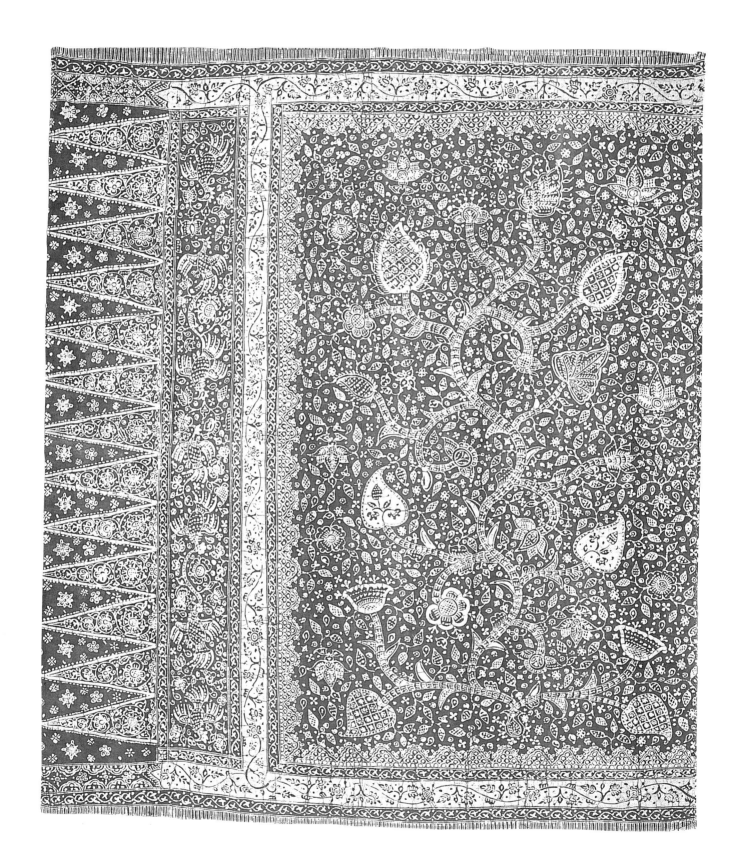

OPPOSITE: A favourite design from Jambi is known as *Batanghari*, the name of the river on which the port of Jambi lies. It is probably derived from the 'tree of life' motif once found on cloths imported from India. The birds in the *papan*, linked by the chain which they both hold in their beaks, suggest that the cloth may have been meant to be worn at a wedding. *Tulis*, cotton. 19th century. 111 x 195 cm. (Kerlogue collection)

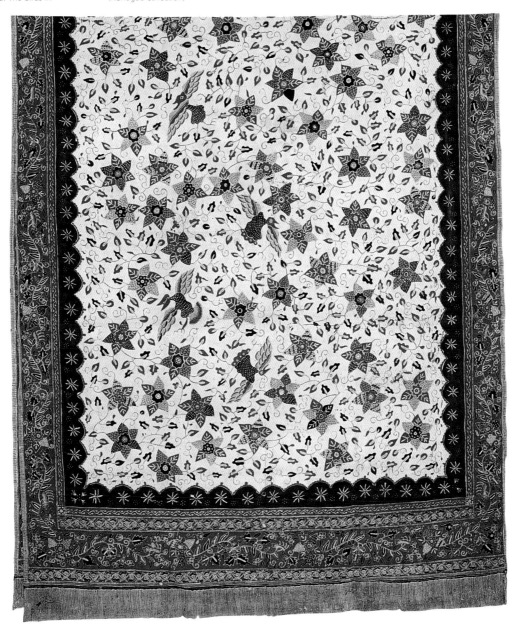

ABOVE: Patterns of flowers arranged asymmetrically over the ground are common in batiks from Sumatra or intended for the Sumatran market. The design is known as '*bunga jatuh*' or '*bunga bertabur*' (fallen or scattered flowers). Flowers are used in a variety of purification ceremonies in Malay Sumatra, for example when a bride is bathed in an infusion of flower petals the night before her marriage. The use of floral motifs is associated with the evanescent power of the perfume. *Tulis*, cotton. 92 x 218 cm. (Kerlogue collection)

One of Jambi's favourite designs is *duren pecah*, or split durian fruit. It is strongly reminiscent of the Javanese *sawat*, but in Jambi the reference to the durian carries more cultural significance than the wings of Garuda's mount. *Tulis*, cotton. Batik Asmah workshop, Olak Kemang, Jambi, 1990s. 111 x 195 cm. (Kerlogue collection)

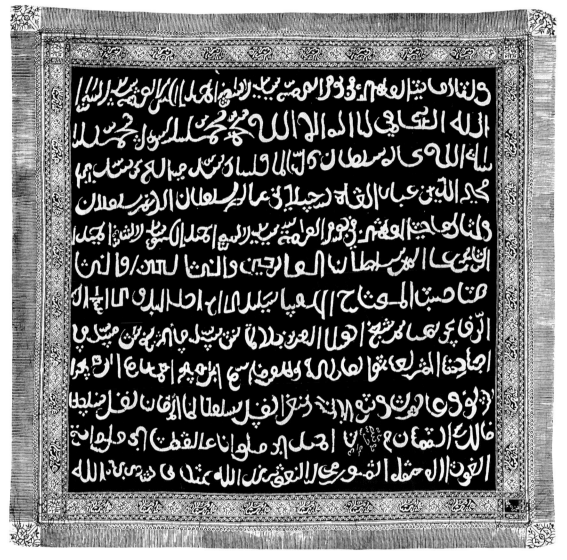

One way in which a cloth could be invested with meaning was by covering it with writing, a task for which the batik technique was eminently suitable. This headcloth is covered with Arabic inscriptions including the *shahadah*, the Muslim profession of faith, and a benediction on the famous Sufi saint Muhyi al-Din 'Abd al-Qadir Jilani. The force is strengthened by the black and white colour scheme which is traditionally thought to have the capacity to ward off evil. *Tulis*, cotton. 93 x 89 cm. (Smend collection)

Banners, vests, men's headcloths, and other cloths covered with Islamic script were perceived as having the power to protect. This cloth is covered with inscriptions in the Arabic language, some derived from the Qur'an, and other talismanic designs. It may have been intended as a headcloth, a cover for the Qur'an or for some other apotropaic purpose. *Tulis*, cotton. Early 20th century. 83.5 x 88.5 cm (Smend collection)

The designs on this cloth speak
clearly of Islam. The link with the
wider Islamic world is indicated by
the repeated swirling *tughra*
motif, derived from the signatures
of the Ottoman rulers. The
calligraphic bands represent holy
phrases from the Qur'an. The
design also includes depictions of
the Dhu'l-Faqar, the double
bladed sword of Ali, son-in-law of
the prophet Mohammed.
Tulis, cotton. Early 20th century.
90 x 220 cm. (Smend collection)

FOLLOWING PAGES: Figures of Dutch soldiers were a popular subject amongst European customers in the 19th and early 20th centuries. These designs were often referred to as 'kompani', a reference to the *VOC* (Dutch East India Company). The Dutch traded in Java for 200 years before assuming direct control around 1820–30. *Kain panjang.* Cap, cotton. Pasisir, late 19th to early 20th century. 105 x 242 cm. (Smend collection)

The design of pairs of geese appears frequently in calligraphic batik and may refer to the origin story of Jambi, Sumatra. The site on which the city was founded is said to have been determined by two geese, which settled there on the river bank. The formation of Islamic script into the shape of birds occurs frequently in such cloths. Shawl (*khudung*) *Tulis*, cotton. Jambi, for export to West Sumatra, late 19th to early 20th century. 89.5 x 210 cm. (Smend collection)

Modern Influences

At the start of the twentieth century there was increased prosperity in the Dutch East Indies, particularly in Java. More people could afford to wear batik or imitation batik, which was being imported from European manufacturers. The production of stamped batik was the key element in coping with the increased demand, and by the early years of the century it had almost entirely replaced hand-drawn *tulis* production. Some European commentators of the day expressed concern that the importation of imitation batik from Europe was adversely affecting Javanese batik production and could eventually render it obsolete. Certainly the introduction of *cap* had transformed the industry in north Javanese centres such as Cirebon and Pekalongan which catered for a growing export market as well as meeting local demand.

The beginnings of industrialization

Where batik had once been a cottage industry, with women working mainly at home, now batik manufactories became the norm. Increasingly, men working away from home formed the largest sector of the workforce. It was men who stamped the cloth with the heavy metal *cap*. Men were taking over the dyeing process too. By 1900 synthetic dyes had begun to be imported into Java

OPPOSITE: Peacocks became very popular in batik designs of the late 19th and early 20th century. They continue to be used as motifs in contemporary batik, especially in centres on the north coast. *Tulis*, cotton. 105.5 x 231.5 cm. (Smend collection)

from Europe, so that the range of colours increased. The new bright hues were especially popular with Chinese customers, and, although there were many technical problems at first, with the artificial dyes liable to fade, gradually more manufacturers adopted the new dyestuffs. Artificial substitutes for beeswax were also introduced, while the range of designs increased. Patterns which had once been reserved for royalty were now replicated on factory-produced cloth so that anyone could wear them.

Batik-making centres developed mainly in the big cities of Java, where the high density of the population meant that markets were readily available. Much of the Javanese batik industry was by now in the hands of Chinese and Arab entrepreneurs, who dominated the supply of raw materials as well as the marketing of the finished cloths. In 1910 the Sarekat Dagang Islam trade association was set up to further the interests of indigenous Muslim enterprises, but these were for the most part much smaller concerns than the Chinese and Arab businesses and they failed to compete in the marketplace. By this time, the Dutch were beginning to adopt an ethical stance towards their colonial subjects. Reports of investigations into conditions in the factories revealed that women workers were obliged to endure long hours spent in stuffy, poorly lit rooms filled with fumes. The male *cap* workers were better off, and although the government made efforts to improve the lot of the female workers, these were of limited effectiveness.

Wars and economic crises

The years which followed were marked by fluctuating demand for batik. During World War I the importation of the cotton cloth for batik making from Dutch cotton mills declined, causing the price of batiks to rise. After the war, the import of Dutch imitation batiks stopped, while the import of cotton cloth resumed and the batik industry revived. The world economic crisis of 1923 also affected the batik industry. Work opportunities on the rubber and sugar plantations declined, and efforts were made to develop rural enterprises such as batik making. In 1921 the Bandung Institute of Textiles had been established, and training programmes organized to instruct workers in weaving, dyeing, design and

business management. In 1929 a Batik Research Centre was set up in Yogyakarta to provide support specifically for the batik industry, especially in relation to the use of new equipment and materials. However, despite a temporary boom in batik production resulting from regulations which protected it from foreign imports, the continuation of the Depression into the 1930s eventually saw local demand plummet. Exports to Thailand and Singapore also declined dramatically during the 1920s. Batik workers could be laid off at short notice, and employment in the batik industry was never a wholly reliable source of income.

One notable exception to this trend was the Fuji factory, set up in 1920 to produce batik cloths for export to Japan. These fabrics were known as '*obi*': long cloths which were folded into sashes and worn above the waist over kimonos particularly by Japanese women. Initially the *obi* produced at the factory were made from silk, but later cotton *obi* were also produced. As production grew, the factory diversified its products. Cotton wall hangings decorated with batik designs were made for sale in Java. This specialization in products meant that the Fuji factory did not suffer during the Depression and in 1927 the factory was still employing about 90 people.

The overall effect of the Depression on the batik industry was that efforts were concentrated on the production of low-quality stamped batik using low-grade cotton fabric. By now, this cambric cloth was being produced locally, though cheap imported material from Japan had become the most commonly used fabric for batik. The Dutch East Indies government responded by introducing a quota system for the import of bleached and unbleached cotton cloth for the batik industry to protect Dutch interests. This resulted in a rise in the price of cloth in Java which forced up the price of finished batik *sarung*, and again the demand for the cloths fell.

During this period, the establishment of batik cooperatives had played a considerable part in the development of the industry. Although it had been suppressed by the Dutch, who wanted to protect their own production, the Sarekat Dagang Islam now served as a model for other organizations, such as the Cooperative of Surakarta Batik Enterprises (PPBS) which was established in Solo in 1935. Not long afterwards, batik enterprises in Yogyakarta followed suit with the formation of a

Cooperative of National Batik Enterprises (PPBBP). Other batik-making centres set up similar associations over the next few years, all aimed at enabling members to obtain supplies directly from importers and ultimately to set up their own factories for the manufacture of cambric. Although foreign imports continued to play a major part, the cooperative movement gained some measure of success.

During World War II the supply of raw materials such as cambric was again disrupted. The period of Japanese occupation from 1942 to 1945 adversely affected both the market for, and the production of, European-style batik. Anti-European feelings were encouraged and many Indo-European families were interned, including a number of the families which had run batik manufactories on the north coast. Although this marked the end of the Indo-European batik enterprises, the styles which these families had pioneered were taken over by Chinese entrepreneurs. This period also saw the emergence of the so-called '*batik Jawa Hokokai*', an extremely intricate ornamental style of batik, with new colour combinations inspired by Japanese taste and commissioned by wealthy Japanese connoisseurs of batik.

Independence and a new national style

Shortages of cambric continued to affect the batik industry in the years of struggle following the departure of the Japanese. After independence, which was declared in 1945 though not secured until 1949, the Indonesian government made efforts to revive and develop batik, both as an economic force and as a symbol of Indonesian nationhood. All the existing cooperatives in Java were brought together under one umbrella organization, the Union of Indonesian Batik Cooperatives (GKBI) in an effort to pool purchasing resources and squeeze out foreign competition. The GKBI set up a company to import cambrics for its members in 1949 and in 1952 it was granted exclusive distribution rights. However, it took some time for this policy to be successful. By this time, batik had come to be seen by many as backward and out of keeping with aspirations towards modernity. Batik's history as an indicator of status was also at odds with the democratic thrust of the new nation. However, a revival did take place, which built on the creation of a new 'national' style of batik.

The proliferation of cooperative organizations had encouraged the setting up of large numbers of small-scale batik enterprises at village level. The coarse batik produced in these workshops, some of it on handwoven cotton cloth, was decorated with a range of designs collectively known as 'Batik Rakyat' (People's Batik) which appealed to popular taste. At the other end of the spectrum, President Soekarno encouraged the creation of a new style of finely drawn batik by the designer K. R. T. Hardjonagoro in Solo. This new style combined popular north coast colour schemes with elements of the courtly designs of Central Java to create a new national style. Soekarno called this style 'Batik Indonesia'. It was taken up with enthusiasm by the large batik manufacturers, and has dominated the market for everyday wear ever since.

Chinese enterprises continued to dominate the batik industry, however, including the trade in raw materials, and especially in the Central Javanese cities of Solo (Surakarta) and Yogyakarta. The two huge manufacturing and distribution firms, Batik Keris and Batik Semar, which together provided the bulk of batik output from 1960 onwards, were both backed by Chinese capital. Silkscreened imitation batik production—introduced during this period and using no resist process at all—was similarly based at a few large factories, though not all of these were Chinese owned.

Batik production now operates in a number of different systems. In some places batik is produced as *kain panjang* by skilled artisans for the high art market, and this handmade high-quality batik is now acquired by collectors and museums, by wealthy women for ceremonial wear or by art lovers to hang on the walls of their homes. There is also a mass-production system for producing textiles as clothing using a semi-skilled workforce controlled by a small number of Javanese, Chinese and multinational investors.

In smaller centres, however, production has continued much as before. The printing of wax with *cap* was never introduced to Madura and only reached Jambi in the 1980s. Similarly, artificial dyes did not replace natural dyes everywhere, and some vegetable dyes are still used in small-scale production in these outlying batik centres. As batik designers and entrepreneurs continue to respond to social, political and economic change, the industry continues to thrive in the modern era.

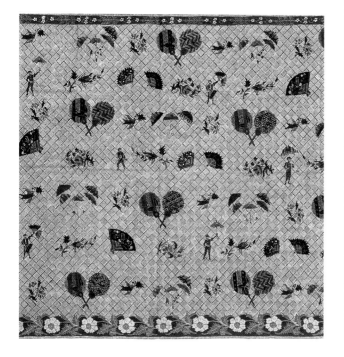

ABOVE: The first Indo-European woman to establish a batik enterprise in Java was Carolina Josephina von Franquemont, in 1840. The most well-known, however, is probably Eliza van Zuylen, whose workshop flourished between 1890 and 1940 and whose signature appears on this piece. The bouquet became a recurrent motif, closely identified with Pekalongan, and persists in contemporary batik. *Sarung. Tulis*, cotton. Signed E. v. Zuylen, Pekalongan. 107 x 190 cm. (Smend collection)

LEFT: Another Indo-European manufacturer who helped to establish the market for motifs with European resonance was Mrs. Lien Metzelaar. The distinctly European motifs of fans and figures holding umbrellas set against a basket-weave ground and the red floral border would have appealed to the Indo-European community. The colour scheme of this cloth shows that artificial dyes were not yet in use. Part of *badan* of *sarung. Tulis*, cotton. Signed L. Metz. Pek., late 19th to 20th century. 105.5 x 214 cm. (Smend collection)

OPPOSITE TOP: One of the first manufacturers to sign her work was Mrs. A. F. Jans, who was the only maker born of Dutch parents. After the death of her husband, she changed her signature to Wed. J. Jans ('Wed.' indicating her widowhood). From 1900 she signed J. Jans as she had before. *Sarung. Tulis*, cotton. Signed J. Jans, late 19th to early 20th century. 105 x 205 cm. (Smend collection)

OPPOSITE BOTTOM: At some point between 1911 and 1915 Mrs. Jans sold her workshop, her recipes and the rights to use her signature to Mrs. Wiler, who later passed them on to Jacqueline van Ardenne. This *sarung*, with a larger signature and simpler work, was probably made during this later period. *Tulis*, cotton. Signed J. Jans, early 20th century. 105.5 x 214 cm. (Smend collection)

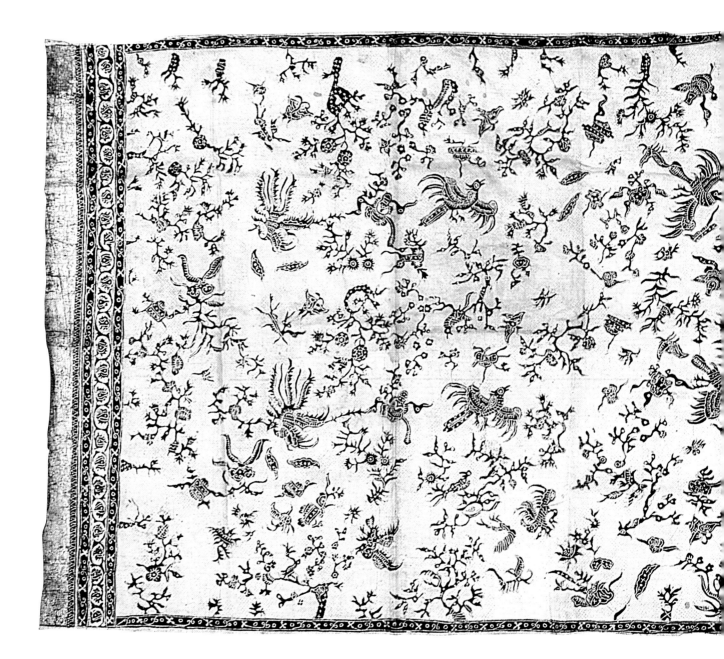

Many batiks produced in Java were embellished with gold leaf and so were waxed on only one side. Some were used locally, as part of a bridal costume. Others, however, were for the Sumatran or Balinese market, like this one, which was collected in Klungkung in Bali. It was probably used as part of a dancer's costume. *Selendang prada. Tulis*, cotton. First half of the 20th century. 84 x 210 cm. (Smend collection)

The *Taman Terate* or 'lotus garden' theme came into batik fashion about 1900, introduced through European magazines when Japanese art was in vogue in Europe. This design of cranes wading was introduced at the turn of the century by Mrs. Lien Metzelaar. There is a multi-flowered bouquet in the *kepala* which dates the cloth to 1910 or later. *Tulis*, cotton. Signed L. Metz Pek. Pekalongan. Early 20th century. 107 x 195 cm. (Smend collection)

The 'lotus garden' design was adopted by many other manufacturers, including makers of Chinese origin. This *sarung*, with both wading and flying cranes, is signed by Phoa Tjong Ling. *Tulis*, cotton. Pekalongan. 106 x 198 cm. (Smend collection)

OPPOSITE TOP: The unusual division of the kepala on this sarung, with its lively pattern of peacocks, suggests that it was made for a European customer. Tulis, cotton, natural dyes. Initialled S.H.C. Pekalongan, early 20th century. 103 x 198.5 cm. (Smend collection)

OPPOSITE BOTTOM: This tiga negeri sarung is described as Buket galaran, 'Buket' being a reference to the bouquet design, while 'galaran' refers to the vertical bands in the badan. Tulis, cotton. Signed Liem Soei Hong, Batang, ca. 1920. 105.5 x 199 cm. (Smend collection)

This sarung with a design of huge butterflies was produced by The Tie Siet of Pekalongan, who ran a flourishing business from 1920 until the 1950s. His children continued to use his signature when they took over the business. Diagonal bands in the kepala had been introduced in the 1890s. Sarung dlorong kupu-kupu. Tulis, cotton. 1920s. 108 x 202.5 cm. (Smend collection)

Although artificial dyes were available from the turn of the century, it was some time before they were widely used. Chinese manufacturers experimented until they had perfected the techniques required, but few Indo-European manufacturers made much use of chemical dyes. Eliza van Zuylen was an exception. *Tulis*, cotton. Signed E. v. Zuylen, Pekalongan, 1930s. 107 x 196 cm. (Smend collection)

TOP: Children's *sarungs*, made for European and Eurasian children, were often of very high quality. Even though it is half the size of an adult's *sarung*, no concession has been made in the scale of the design in this example. *Tulis*, cotton. Early 20th century. 59 x 105 cm. (Smend collection)

BOTTOM: *Sarungs* in blue on a cream ground are known as *sarung kelengan*, and amongst Peranakan wearers were appropriate for women in mourning. However, the lotus flowers and buds, and the butterflies and birds approaching them to sip the nectar, suggest that in this case the colour merely shows that it is intended for an older woman, the motifs perhaps suggesting the promise of new life elsewhere in the family. Signed The Tie Siet, Pekalongan. *Tulis*, cotton. 107 x 206 cm. (Smend collection)

OPPOSITE: M. Coenraad moved to Pacitan from Surakarta around 1880 and set up a batik manufactory with her sister. Most of their batiks were dyed in indigo and *soga*, as is this one. *Tulis*, cotton. Signed M. Coenraad, Patjitan, late 19th or early 20th century. 107.5 x 202 cm. (Smend collection)

OPPOSITE TOP: *Sarungs* bearing the signature Simonet, as this one does, are the work of Tan Ien Nio, who married Jacobus Simonet in 1890. She closed her workshop in 1930. Her customers were mainly European or Indo-European, and the motifs and colour schemes were chosen to appeal to them. *Tulis*, cotton. Pekalongan, ca. 1910. 107 x 205.5 cm. (Smend collection)

OPPOSITE BOTTOM: A *kain panjang* arranged in the Indo-European style, with a *booh* (bow) border along the lower edge and one vertical side only. *Tulis*, cotton. Signed Simonet, Pekalongan, ca. 1910. 105 x 229.5 cm. (Smend collection)

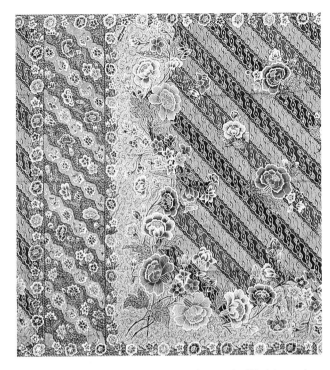

An example of the intense colours and textures of *Jawa Hokokai* batik design. *Tulis*, cotton. Signed Oey Kheng Liem, Pekalongan, 1941. 109.5 x 208 cm. (Smend collection)

Cotton was extremely scarce during World War II, and batik was produced only for those who could afford it. The Japanese style *Jawa Hokokai* was thus extremely detailed. It was often produced in *pagi-sore* format. *Tulis*, cotton. Pekalongan, early 1940s. 109 x 263.5 cm. (Smend collection)

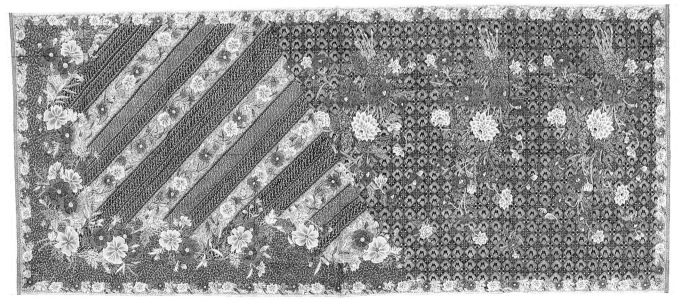

Raden Tumenggung Hardjonagoro
(Go Tik Swan) came from a family
of batik manufacturers, but
entered the field rather late,
encouraged by President
Soekarno, the first president of
independent Indonesia. In the
1950s it was Hardjonagoro who
came up with the new Batik
Indonesia style, which brought
together and largely replaced
regional forms of batik. *Pisan Bali.*
Tulis, cotton, chemical dyes.
Surakarta, 1997. 102 x 244 cm.
(Willach collection)

OPPOSITE TOP: Batik manufacturers
continue to innovate to suit the
demands of today's market.
Research at the Batik Research
Institute in Yogyakarta has led to
widespread use of silk as a base
fabric in recent years, and designers
invent new styles, using the ever
growing range of colours which
can be achieved. *Sarung. Tulis*,
chemical dyes on handwoven silk.
Danar Hadi, Surakarta, 2001.
114 x 254 cm. (Willach collection)

OPPOSITE BOTTOM: Some village
cooperatives produce very high
quality work. This *kain panjang* is
from one such enterprise in
Giroloyo, in the Bantul region of
Yogyakarta. *Keong sari.*
Tulis, chemical dyes. 2000.
101 x 240 cm. (Willach collection)

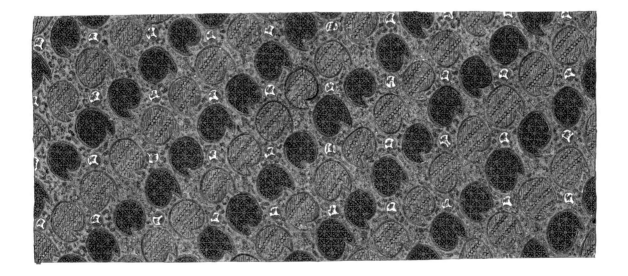

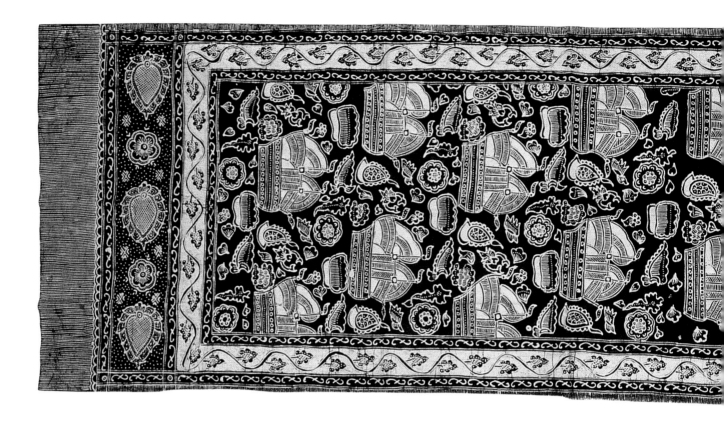

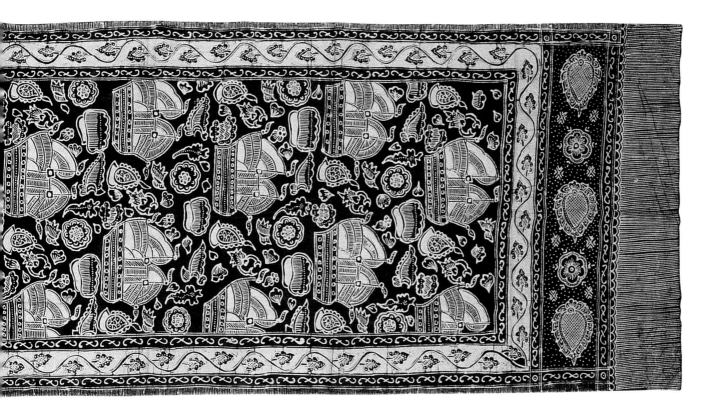

TOP: Historical events sometimes provide inspiration for batik designs, as in this Jambi design called *Kapal Sanggat*, or 'ship aground'. Ships frequently ran aground in the shallow waters of the Batanghari river on which the city was built, often resulting in an unexpected windfall for the inhabitants. *Kapal Sanggat* is a popular design, which has now been adopted as the symbol of Jambi municipality. *Selendang*. Batik Asmah workshop, Olak Kemang, Jambi. *Tulis*, cotton. 1994. 51 x 205.5 cm. (Kerlogue collection)

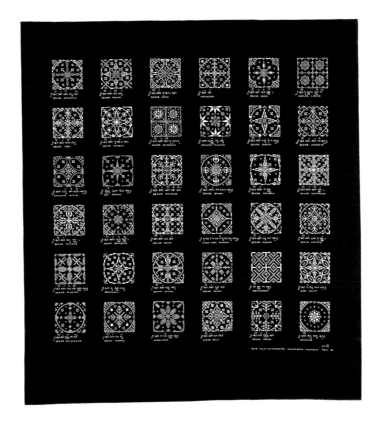

OPPOSITE: *Ceplok medali*. The design of this batik, made by a member of the family of the sultan of Yogyakarta, represents a medallion once worn by her grandfather on his jacket. Made by Ibu Hambardjan Prawirojuwono. *Tulis*, cotton, chemical dyes. Yogyakarta, 2000. 103 x 240 cm. (Willach collection)

There has long been a tradition of making samplers of batik designs. This modern example made up of *nitik* motifs, which imitate the effect of weaving, shows how contemporary makers are recording traditional motifs to preserve them for future generations. It is the work of Hani Winotosastro from Yogyakarta, using natural indigo on cotton. *Tulis*, cotton. Recent. 90 x 95 cm. (Willach collection)

Kain panjang with a variant of
the *parang* motif in different
sizes. *Tulis*, cotton. Yogyakarta.
106 x 260 cm. (Smend collection)

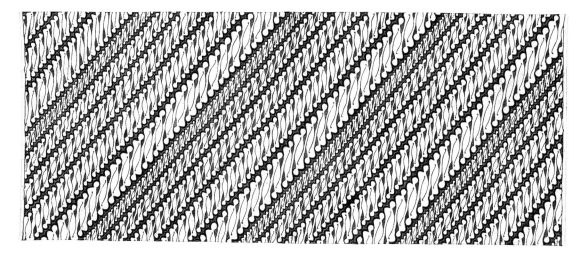

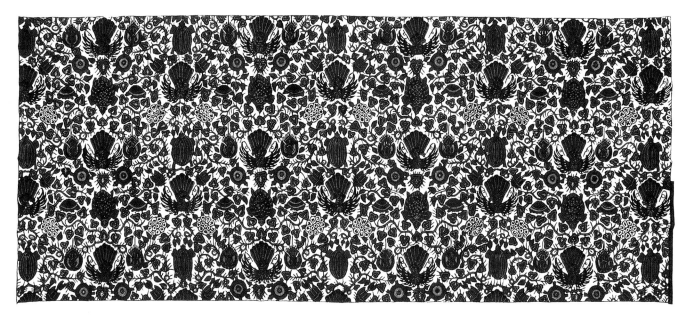

Kain semen burontoyo latar petak.
This fine piece was produced at
the batik workshop attached to
the palace in Yogyakarta. It is
signed by the maker, Ibu Hadi

Subroto, who drew the wax on
by hand. Yogyakarta. *Tulis*,
cotton, chemical dyes.
105 x 250 cm. (Willach collection)

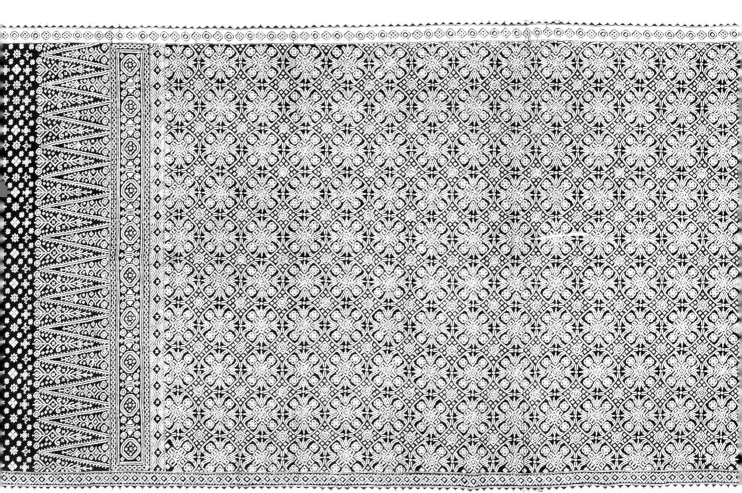

The continuity of some batik
designs is remarkable. The
jelamprang design had once
embellished the silk *patola* cloths
favoured for use at court which
had been imported to Indonesia
for at least 500 years. In Yogyakarta,
it is known as '*nitik caka*'.
Tulis, cotton. Pekalongan.
108.5 x 272.5 cm. (Smend collection)

Sawat penganten. Wall hanging.
Tulis, cotton, chemical dyes.
Produced by Masina, Trusmi,
Cirebon, 1994. 101 x 101 cm.
(Willach collection)

OPPOSITE: *Kain semen gurdo latar
ireng*. The stately monumentality
of the Central Javanese batik
tradition is evident in this *kain
panjang*, an ancient design in
colours which depart a little from
those of old. *Tulis*, cotton,
chemical dyes. Produced by
R. Ayu Hambardjan, Yogyakarta,
2001. 103 x 240 cm.
(Willach collection)

There is growing interest in
reviving the use of natural dyes
in Indonesian batik-making. This
silk *selendang*, produced by
Kerajinan Batik Winotosastro, was
dyed in natural indigo and *soga*,
although the design is distinctly
modern. *Tulis*, silk. Signed by Hani
Winotosastro, Yogyakarta.
56 x 244 cm. (Willach collection)

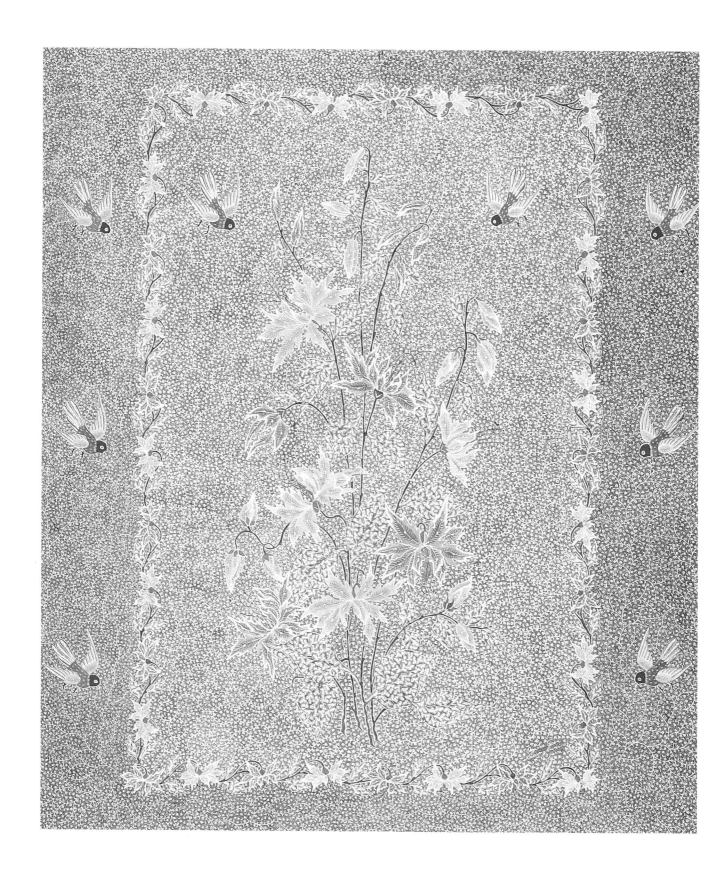

OPPOSITE: There is still a market for the almost unbelievably fine work produced by a few highly skilled makers in Kedungwuni on the north coast. This wall hanging is based on a traditional *sarung* design using the pastel colours and tones traditionally favoured by women of Chinese descent. Small fields of colour are applied to the cloth with the brush, *coletan*, or by rubbing in a dye paste. *Tulis* and *colet*, cotton. Signed Oey Soe Tjoen, Kedungwuni, recent. 105 x 96 cm. (Willach collection)

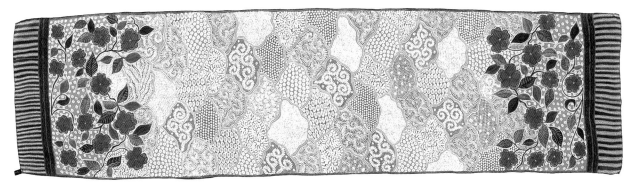

TOP AND BOTTOM: Matching *kain* and *selendang* have always been popular for formal wear. This set, with its rich red flowers set against a pale and delicate ground, is in *crêpe de chine*, and was designed by one of the most prominent batik artists of the day, Ardiyanto Pranata. *Tulis*, silk. Yogyakarta, 1995. *Kain.*112 x 252 cm. *Selendang.* 51 x 206 cm. (Smend collection)

FOLLOWING PAGES: A multitude of human figures are hidden amongst the fruits and flowers in this 20th-century interpretation of the *alas-alasan* (forest) design, known as *Kain Fantasi*. *Tulis*, cotton. Central Java. 107 x 247 cm. (Smend collection)

Batik as Costume

The use of batik as costume did not become widespread in Indonesia until relatively recent times. Many centuries ago most of the peoples of the Indonesian archipelago wore cloth, coarsely woven from handspun fibres, on the lower part of their body. Those textiles which had decorative elements were probably used mainly for ritual and ceremony, and elaborately designed costume was only worn by the more prestigious members of the community. The batik technique, where it existed, was likely to have been used to draw magical symbols on items such as coverings for ceremonial offerings of food, cloths for healing ceremonies or ritual blankets such as the *kain* *simbut* once used in parts of West Java. Those peoples who did produce their own decorated cloth for clothing chiefly used the warp *ikat* technique, still practised by many of the peoples of the eastern islands, especially in the production of textiles for gift exchanges and for wearing at weddings.

Textiles imported from India in past centuries were important markers of status and the most costly of these were restricted, through their high cost or by decree, to those in positions of power. The double-*ikat patola*, imported from India since at least the thirteenth century and probably much earlier, was by far the most prestigious of these cloths. Written texts from the seventeenth century frequently refer the use of these high-status cloths by Javanese nobles at court and in battle. Batik does not seem to have been introduced as part of court costume in Java until later. The Hindu Majapahit court, which had held power over much of the region until that time, had fallen and the disruption to trade which accompanied its demise and the period of Islamization which followed may have led to the replacement of costly *patolu* by locally produced batik.

Outside the courts, simple forms of batik may have been produced on village clothing, but even as late as the nineteenth century it seems that batik was rarely used as everyday wear by ordinary folk except in those places where cheap imported cloth was not available. Not until the mid-nineteenth century did locally produced batik become sufficiently inexpensive to rival cloths imported from India, and later from Europe, as everyday attire for the majority of the population. However, after that time batik became the most important material, especially for women's clothing, and despite the challenge from Western styles of clothing such as jeans and T-shirts, batik—and imitations of batik—remains a central element in the attire of the people of Indonesia.

Traditional forms

Traditionally, the batiks used for costume were rectangles of cloth, wrapped or draped around the body according to their function. Batik lengths for skirt cloths were sewn into tubes as *sarung* or left unsewn in longer lengths as *kain panjang*. *Kain panjang* are still worn today, especially in Central Java, for formal occasions and traditional ceremonies. Worn by women, they form part of the recognized national costume of Indonesia. *Sarung* are more common in the coastal areas and outer islands where they are worn for less formal occasions, mostly by women but also sometimes by men. *Selendang* are used primarily as shawls, usually by women. Men's headcloths, once common throughout the Indo-Malay world, are now worn mainly for ceremonies where they sometimes still signify the status of the wearer. Other traditional forms of batik costume, now rarely seen, include the *kemben*, *dodot* and *sampur*.

Sarung

Sarung are usually about a metre wide and 2.25 metres long. The two ends are sewn together to form a tube. It is worn around the lower part of the body, folded and tucked in at the waist. The *sarung* always features a characteristic design element known as the *kepala*, or head, an area of the design roughly a third of the length of the cloth where the pattern differs from the main ground pattern in the rest of the cloth. Many of these *kepala* are characterized by two rows of triangles, known in Java as '*pucuk rebung*', or bamboo shoots. This part of the *kepala* is the *tumpal*. To either side of the *tumpal* are the *papan*, vertical panels which separate the *tumpal* from the *badan*, the main body of the cloth. Running horizontally along the top and bottom of the *sarung* there is normally a narrow decorative border. Some *sarung* may have a different pattern in the *kepala*; for example, *sarung* made for the Indo-European or Chinese communities often replaced the distinctive triangles with a bouquet of flowers. In Madura, the *kepala* is frequently composed of several diagonal rows of waves, referred to as '*Tase Malaya*', the Malayan Sea, each row being decorated with a different filling pattern.

The *kepala* may be situated at one end of the *sarung*, in the middle or somewhere in between, and this can sometimes give a clue as to the age of a batik or its place of origin. However, once the cloth has been sewn into a tube it makes no difference where the *kepala* is situated. What is important is where it is worn: usually at the front of the body or to one side. Different regions have different conventions in this respect. Among men it is more likely to be worn to the rear.

Kain panjang

The *kain panjang*, sometimes just called a *kain*, is of the same width as a *sarung*, but of greater length. It is not sewn into a tube but left free at the ends. The *kain* is wrapped around the lower body, in a clockwise direction for women, or anti-clockwise for men. It is usually folded or pleated to fit and fastened by tucking in at the waist. In the palaces of Central Java, the ladies of the court had their own way of folding the *kain panjang*. Instead of pleating and tucking, the end of the *kain* would either be folded back on itself in the opposite direction to the way it was originally wrapped, or it might be pulled in and left to drape in a gentle frill down the right-hand side of the body.

The composition of the design of a *kain panjang* differs from that of a *sarung*. In a *kain panjang*, the *kepala* is usually split into two, with one row of *tumpal* triangles at each end. If both ends have the same motif, each end may be dyed in a different colour and the cloth is then referred to as '*pagi-sore*' (morning–afternoon). In some areas, the two ends feature different motifs. For example, in Indramayu it is common for one end to have the traditional *tumpal* design consisting of one row of large triangles and a *papan*, while the other is finished with just a small row of tiny triangles.

Selendang

The *selendang*, or shawl, probably developed from a loose cloth hung over the shoulder to perform various functions in the past: as a sling for carrying a baby or other burden, as a covering for the breasts, or to protect the head from the sun when necessary. It is now common to wear a matching pair of *kain panjang* and *selendang* for formal occasions, but this custom was introduced only a few decades ago. Among communities where Islamic dress codes are strong, *selendang* are comparatively large and are used to cover both head and shoulders, though a *sarung* may be used to serve this purpose.

In Central Java, the *selendang* is generally around 1.5 metres long and just under 0.5 metres wide. In eastern Sumatra it is

The patchwork worn by these Tengger priests is testimony to its use in religious contexts. It may be that the *tambal* design derives from the belief that its use imbued the wearer with spiritual power or purity. Photographer unknown, ca. 1880. (Leo Haks photo collection, Amsterdam)

roughly the same length but double the width, reflecting its use as a head covering. In some places, special *selendang* known as '*gendongan*' are made to carry babies; these are often much longer than ordinary *selendang*, as is the case in the Tuban area.

Two variations of the *selendang* appear in the costume of dancers in Central Java. One is the *sampur*, a long narrow cloth which the dancer uses to wave and flick in graceful movements as part of his or her expressive vocabulary. The *sampur* is one of the elements of dress which owes its origins to *patolu* cloths, and the design is usually made up of patterns and colours reminiscent of the *ikat* silks worn at court in the past.

Female dancers also wear *kemben*, as do brides on their wedding day. The *kemben* is a long narrow cloth wrapped around the upper part of the body. Many are decorated with the *tritik* and *jumputan* techniques, in which the dye is resisted not by the use of wax but by sewing the cloth or tying it to make tiny knots before the dyeing process. Those which

Woman wearing a *kain*. Photographer unknown, ca. 1880.
(Leo Haks photo collection, Amsterdam)

are decorated with batik usually have a plain lozenge or rectangle in the centre, edged on the inside with the *lidah api*, or 'tongues of flame', motif.

Headcloths

The headcloths worn by men, known as *destar* or *iket kepala*, are usually around a metre square with the design arranged symmetrically on the cloth. Some headcloths have a square in the centre, set diagonally against the main frame of the cloth. These are known as *iket tengahan*. Others may be decorated with an all-over pattern, or the design may be different on the diagonally opposed halves of the cloth.

Throughout the archipelago, batik headcloths were used by men in traditional ceremonies. In some cases they were regarded as containing protective power, especially those embellished with phrases from the Qur'an in Arabic script. Often they were folded into shapes which indicated status or rank. Even today there are many places and occasions when a batik headcloth is a necessary part of formal attire.

Dodot

The *dodot* is a huge cloth, usually 3.5 to 4 metres long and 2 to 2.5 metres wide. In Central Java it is often worn around the waist at wedding ceremonies by both bride and groom, especially members of the nobility. Members of the royal family would also wear *dodot* at certain ceremonies, and *bedoyo* and *serimpi* court dancers might also wear them.

In the centre of the *dodot* is a large empty lozenge, or *tengahan*, sometimes lined with silk. In the main body the pattern is likely to be one of the motifs reserved for members of the king's immediate family, and known as *larangan* (forbidden). Reserved for the king himself was the *dodot bangun tulak alas-alasan*, a design believed to have magical protective properties. In this cloth the centre is white or cream, while the outer area is decorated with the *alas-alasan* motif in blue-black. Often the surface of the cloth is embellished with gold leaf (*perada*), accentuating the leafy patterns of the *alas-alasan*, or forest design. The white centrefield is said to represent a pool, fed by a spring in its exact centre. The king—regarded in traditional Javanese thought as the centre of the universe, its navel or axis—is thus wrapped symbolically in the source of water which radiates life to the people. Although this type of *dodot* should be worn only by the king, there is an exception to this rule. On their wedding day, bride and groom are symbolically regarded as king and queen for the day, a role sometimes expressed by their wearing of this special design.

The *dodot* can be worn folded into a variety of shapes, reflecting the status of the wearer. If it is rucked up to right and left, the height of the ruck corresponds with the wearer's rank. There is usually also a part which hangs down, the *kanco*, and the length to which this falls also depends on the status of the wearer; for the king this part will sweep along the floor, whereas for courtiers it does not touch the ground.

Modern developments in costume

The use of batik as costume has never been static, and batik has been used in many other forms over the last several centuries. Regional variations occur too: in Jambi, for example, it was common in the late nineteenth century for the woman's *baju kurung*, or long tunic, to be made of locally produced batik with simple symmetrical motifs in white set against a blue background.

European residents in the Dutch East Indies also adapted local costume to meet their own taste and requirements. Until the last decades of colonial rule, men often had trousers made up in batik for casual wear at home, though many also wore *sarung* to keep them cooler in the evenings. As the colonial period came to an end, it was the indigenous population which rejected batik as attire for men. Some wished to express their allegiance to the modern world and their sense of status by adopting European jackets and trousers; others turned to Arabic styles to declare themselves as members of the Islamic world, opposed to Western oppression.

After independence, there were several developments in the use of batik. Western styles began to be made up in batik cloth, and there was a resurgence in the use of traditional costume itself. In addition, loose-fitting shifts for women began to be made for lounging in at home. For men, short-sleeved shirts in batik became popular, modelled on the Hawaiian shirt. However, not until batik began to be made by the bolt was it possible to tailor dresses for women in batik fabrics.

The credit for developing batik as a national costume is usually given to Indonesia's first president, Soekarno. He was instrumental in encouraging the creation of new designs, especially for the batik worn by women on formal occasions. It was Ali Sadikin, the governor of Jakarta, however, who was chiefly responsible for the introduction of long-sleeved batik shirts as formal wear for men, in 1972. His declaration that such wear was appropriate was endorsed by President Soeharto and long-sleeved batik shirts quickly became recognized as part of the national costume for men, alongside the *kain panjang* and the *kebaya*, a long tight-fitting blouse, for women.

At the start of the 1970s it became possible to make batik using artificial dyes on silk without damaging the fabric. Silk batik quickly became the choice for fashionable ladies and for men. At first the fabric used was imported from China and then from other countries. Later the trend provided impetus for an indigenous silk industry.

By the early 1980s the range of silk fabrics, as well as the range of colours available, had grown enormously. Batik as the material of choice for glamorous evening wear became increasingly subject to changing fashion trends, in terms of both design and embellishment. Designers such as Iwan Tirta explored new avenues, incorporating motifs from beyond the court repertoire and making them new by hugely inflating the scale of the motifs, or manipulating them to follow the lines of the garment. Tirta also introduced much larger cloths, such as wide elegant silk *selendangs* to accompany the silk *kain panjang*. Another development in fashion was gold-leaf embellishment, once found only on court textiles, which enjoyed a period of popularity with wealthier women.

The 1980s were characterized by a proliferation of batik fashion shows, at which designers displayed their use of batik for ball gowns, cocktail dresses and other fashions, including those for men. As Indonesia opened its doors to increased foreign investment, the marketing of batik as an export product expanded throughout the world. In particular, scarves and stoles in fine silk gauze became hugely fashionable at an international level. Although the economic crisis of 1997 hit the batik industry hard, batik costume and the batik industry have shown remarkable resilience and remain at the core of Indonesian national identity and pride.

OPPOSITE: Two Balinese women and a boy. The women are wearing *kain* made of batik and breastcloths of other fabrics. Photographer unknown, ca. 1915. (Leo Haks photo collection, Amsterdam)

RIGHT: During the colonial period Indo-Europeans wore batik in combination with European costume elements. It was also used to make household soft furnishings such as tablecloths, a use which continues today. (Leo Haks photo collection, Amsterdam)

BELOW: Dutch residents often wore batik at home, sometimes commissioned from local women. Batik trousers were worn at home by men from many sectors of society. Photographer unknown, ca. 1925. (Leo Haks photo collection, Amsterdam)

LEFT: A Javanese child minder wearing a *sarung* with a *garis miring* design. Photographer unknown, ca. 1920. (Leo Haks photo collection, Amsterdam)

OPPOSITE: Headcloths worn by Javanese men were tied in a variety of styles indicative of the court with which they were associated and their rank. The triangular flap at the front is a *kuncung*, and suggests they are from Yogyakarta. Kassian Cephas, ca. 1890. (Yu-Chee Chong Fine Art, London)

BELOW: Pangeran Jayakusuma of the Mangkunegara court wearing one of the *parang rusak* family of designs, motifs which signify power and are reserved at court for the highest echelons of the aristocracy. Photographer unknown, ca. 1860. (Yu-Chee Chong Fine Art, London)

A local ruler in Yogyakarta with wife and child. The wife's *kain* is folded at the front into small pleats in typical Central Javanese style. Gahin, 1927. (Leo Haks photo collection, Amsterdam)

Regent of Pemalang and his wife. The trousers appear to be made from *patola* cloth; the *dodot* hangs in folds from his waist. The height of the cloth from the ground is a measure of his rank. Riechan, 1930. (Leo Haks photo collection, Amsterdam)

A Javanese prince from the court of Yogyakarta, dressed for a *wayang wong* performance with a sash in a *patola* design. Tassilo Adam or Chenan, 1923–26. (Leo Haks photo collection, Amsterdam)

A prince of Yogyakarta wearing a *dodot* of batik over trousers made from *patola* cloth. Photographer unknown, 1910. (Leo Haks photo collection, Amsterdam)

OPPOSITE: Servant girl with fan. Photographer unknown, ca. 1870. (Leo Haks photo collection, Amsterdam)

RIGHT: The *kepala* of this servant girl's *sarung* is folded and worn at the front. Photographer unknown, ca. 1870. (Leo Haks photo collection, Amsterdam)

BELOW LEFT: Unusually, this girl's *sarung* is loosely gathered at the waist below her jacket. Photographer unknown, ca. 1880. (Leo Haks photo collection, Amsterdam)

BELOW RIGHT: Relaxing in the home and when bathing, women often wear their *sarungs* above their breasts. This girl is so small that despite this, it still reaches to her ankles. Photographer unknown, ca. 1880. (Leo Haks photo collection, Amsterdam)

Girl with Her Dog, Jan D. Beynon,
1873. Oil on canvas, 58 x 44 cm.
Private collection. (Image courtesy
of Haks and Maris, Amsterdam)

Many young women today still
carry their babies in *gendongan*
in a very similar manner to this.
Coloured postcard, ca.1890.
(Leo Haks photo collection,
Amsterdam)

A studio-posed portrait of what appears to be a fairly well-to-do woman. Photographer unknown, ca. 1890. (Leo Haks photo collection, Amsterdam)

The bold *parang* design and gold chain mark the high status of the subject. He is Prince Buminoto, brother of the Sultan of Yogyakarta. Hubert Vos, 1899. Oil on canvas. 198 x 90 cm. Private collection. (Image courtesy of Haks and Maris, Amsterdam)

The sash of the bride and the
trousers of the groom in this
wedding photograph are in a
distinctive *patola* pattern. Both
parents wear batik *kain*, while
bride and groom wear the
aristocratic costume of the
Yogyakarta nobility. Gahin, 1920.
(Leo Haks photo collection,
Amsterdam)

When he sat for this portrait painted by Suparno in 1939, Sultan Hamengkubuwono VIII of Yogyakarta seems to have chosen to be depicted in a pattern which was not reserved for the royal family. Suparno, 1939. Oil on canvas, laid down on panel. 85 x 65 cm. (Haks and Maris, Amsterdam)

Sri Sultan Hamengkubuwono X of Yogyakarta and Ratu Hemas. The batik design which they are both wearing includes an assemblage of royal designs: as well as the *parang* motif, there is the pattern of interlocking circles known as *kawung* and the *sawat*, representing the wings and tail of Garuda.

In traditional *sarungs* such as this one, the *kepala* panel divided the main design field, the *badan*, into two equal parts. The *kepala* shown here is traditional, being made up of rows of opposed triangles (*pucuk rebung*, or bamboo shoots, sometimes known as 'tumpal'), and two vertical *papan* panels. In less traditional formats, the *kepala* is often at one end of the cloth, and the form of the *kepala* may vary considerably. Although this example has been opened out to show how the design is laid out, a *sarung* is always sewn into a tube before it is worn. *Tulis*, cotton. Ca. 1890. 106 x 199 cm. (Smend collection)

Unlike the *sarung*, the *kain panjang* is not sewn into a tube, but folded at the waist to secure it. In Java, the *kain* is often characterized by the absence of the triangular *tumpal* elements, with only a narrow plain border at each end. The arrangement of this elegant piece, with its profusion of flowers and tendrils interspersed with birds, is typical. *Tulis*, cotton. 106.5 x 272.5 cm. (Smend collection)

The division of a *kain panjang* into two halves (*pagi-sore*) by means of a diagonal division allows the wearer to choose which design she wishes to reveal. The *pagi-sore* style is common in Pasisir batiks from Peranakan makers. In this example, pairs of ducks or geese are clear references to marital fidelity, and here are set against a striking black background, swimming amongst long-stemmed trumpet-shaped flowers. In the other half of the cloth the cranes wading amongst lotus flowers while insects buzz around them dwarf those flying in the sky above, suggesting an attempt at perspective on the part of the artist. *Kain panjang pagi-sore. Tulis*, cotton. Sidhoarjo. 105.5 x 274 cm. (Smend collection)

PREVIOUS PAGES: The *dodot* is worn mainly by members of the aristocracy in the Central Javanese courts. It is a huge cloth, often with a central lozenge which is sometimes covered by a fine silk overlay. Its form may have been inspired by Indian trade cloths of similar design. *Dodot. Tulis*, cotton. Yogyakarta. 208.5 x 329 cm. (Smend collection)

OPPOSITE: *Kain panjang* with the two ends in a different colour are typical of Sumatran taste, as is the pale gold of the base cloth of this example. It may have been made in Java for sale in Sumatra. *Tulis*, cotton, vegetal dyes. Late 19th to early 20th century. 106 x 259 cm. (Smend collection)

The larger type of *selendang* worn over the head and shoulders was very popular with Malay women in Sumatra. This one was probably made for export. *Tulis*, cotton. Lasem, first half of the 20th century. 105.5 x 267 cm. (Smend collection)

The *gendongan* is used to carry a
wide variety of goods, and was
once an essential part of every
Javanese household. Nowadays
gendongan are most commonly
used for carrying babies. *Tulis*,
cotton. Pasisir, ca. 1930.
84 x 315.5 cm. (Smend collection)

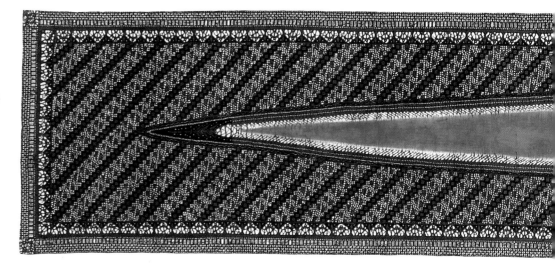

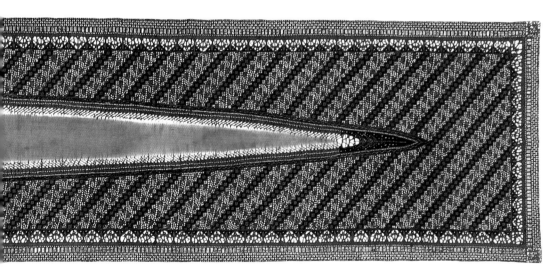

The breastcloth, or *kemben*, is worn at ceremonies, mainly by members of the aristocracy in Central Java. This example, with a blue lozenge, or *tengahan*, at the centre, originated from the Yogyakarta *kraton*. *Tulis*, cotton. 52.5 x 253 cm. (Smend collection)

A headcloth (*iket kepala*) was an essential accoutrement for men in traditional Javanese society. The design of the main field of this headcloth, covered in flowers, leaves and seeds, is an example of the *semen* type of pattern, symbolizing vigour and abundance. The central red *tengahan* is edged with *lidah api*, or 'tongues of flame'. *Tulis*, cotton, natural dyes. 106 x 105 cm. (Smend collection)

The mystical patterns which
cover this finely executed
headcloth seem to suggest the
forms of the Arabic letters for
the word 'Allah', without quite
spelling them out. The cloth was
probably regarded as having
power to protect the wearer.
Tulis, cotton. 20th century.
106 x 105 cm. (Smend collection)

Batik began to be used for
tailored garments in the 19th
century, notably for pyjama
trousers for European men, and
less commonly, sleeping trousers
for boys. These three pairs date
from the early 20th century.
Tulis, cotton. (Smend collection)

BELOW: In the 1980s and 1990s, motifs drawn from a number of traditions, in this case Sumatran *pelangi* designs, were drawn on fine silk for use by fashionable urban women. *Tulis*, silk. Yusman Siswandi, Solo, 1985. 108.5 x 208 cm. (Smend collection)

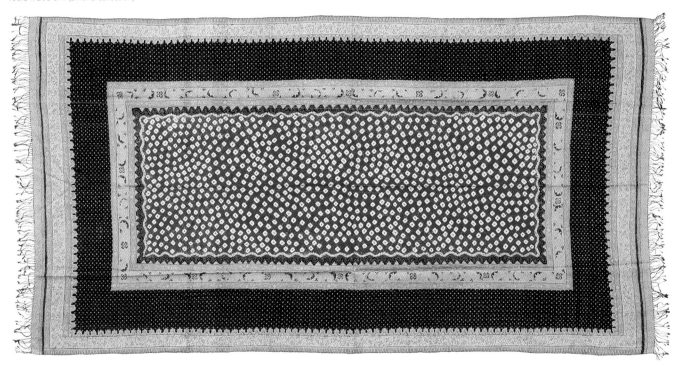

FOLLOWING PAGES: *Kepiting* (crabs). *Tulis*, cotton. Early 20th century. 106.5 x 245 cm. (Smend collection)

Batik in Art

To what extent can traditional forms of batik be regarded as 'art'? Judgments about the quality of batik and the skill of the maker are made every day, but how far these judgements are based on aesthetic criteria and how far they relate to ideas about the quality of artistic expression of the artist is open to question. The terms most frequently used in judging a piece of batik are '*halus*' and '*kasar*'. Put at their simplest, these terms mean 'refined' and 'coarse'. *Batik halus* is smooth and finely executed; *batik kasar* is on rougher cloth and the work is more crude. Lines should be clear and clean (*terang*), strokes should be smooth and flowing, and the overall design should be 'alive' (*hidup*). But these are simplifications.

Many other factors come into play when evaluating a piece of batik. The rank or status of the person who made the batik is important, so that a cloth waxed by the hand of a royal princess would be deemed to have special value and quality regardless of the workmanship. The cloth becomes imbued with the spirit of the woman who worked it and takes on a corresponding spiritual value. On the other hand, a cloth which has been worn by someone of high rank will increase in value, even if the skills which produced it were only moderate.

What of the maker of the piece? Are some makers regarded as artists, while others as merely craftswomen? A traditional *sarung* is rarely made by just one worker:

the waxing of the outline of the design may be undertaken by one person, the fillings by another, the preparation of the cloth, its dyeing and finishing, by more. Thus although a fine batik may bear the name of a maker, it is likely to be the name of the family or workshop which produced it, rather than the name of one artist. A signature is probably that of the workshop owner, who may or may not have played a practical part in the creation of the piece. Designs are likely to be repetitions of well-loved designs passed down the generations. Innovations tend to be small; a combination of existing designs or their rearrangement in the space available. One area where the batik artist can make her own mark is in the *kembangen*, the 'flowering' of the piece. In practice this refers to the *isen*, the filling of the background, which each batik artist accomplishes in accordance with her own aesthetic sense.

Batik painting

While traditional batik work has never really been regarded as an art in the Western tradition, batik painting has come to take its place among the other arts of Indonesia. Many modern chemical dyes can be painted or sprayed onto the cloth in small areas, and this is one of the factors which contributed to the emergence of 'batik painting'. One of the first to experiment with this form was Pak Kuswadji Kawindrasusanto, who had served at one of the Yogyakarta courts in the 1950s as a librarian. In his early work he created depictions of scenes from classical Javanese literature in the blues and browns associated with the royal courts.

In the 1960s, Pak Kuswadji was one of several artists who were invited to take part in a project at the Batik Research Centre in Yogyakarta. The aim of the project was to explore ways of developing the batik industry through creative use of materials and design innovations. Several of the artists involved had trained at the Yogyakarta academy of fine arts (ASRI) and had been used to working in oils and other conventional media. Here experiments were made with new colours and forms, incorporating Western artistic approaches as well as local inspiration. The batik paintings they produced were rectangular compositions on fabric stretched on frames. It was natural that they should incorporate the forms of these other media in their experiments with batik, and in 1965 some

of their batik works were exhibited at the Sonobudoyo Museum in Yogyakarta. Those taking part included Kuswadji's brother, Bagong Kussudiardja, Soelardjo and Abas Alibasyah.

Art and society

The revolution in art reflected changes taking place in Indonesian society in the 1960s, when Indonesia was undergoing a period of unprecedented change. The newly independent republic, reacting against her history of enforced subservience to colonial powers, had at first explored communist ideas. Lekra, the Institute for People's Culture, founded in 1950, had pledged to demolish the remains of colonial culture and repudiated 'the antihuman, antisocial character of the culture that is not-of-the-people'. It supported 'creative initiative, creative daring', and agreed with 'every form, every style, so long as it is faithful to truth and meets the highest standards of artistic beauty'.

One artist who had been a leading member of Lekra was Mohamad Hadi, a painter who became involved in preparing political banners as well as sets and backdrops for theatrical performances of Javanese classic tales. In the early 1960s he and his wife established a batik workshop where he tackled the problem of using a medium whose identity had become so closely associated with the 'feudal' court system. Although Hadi continued to work in the established classical medium of *batik tulis*, producing traditional skirt cloths and making use of traditional designs and dyes, he added a radical political dimension to his work through manipulating the motifs. For example, into the well-established latticework form of *sido mukti* he introduced images such as the two-wheeled ox-cart, the peasant's sunhat and the crossed sickle. The cause of peasant women was promoted by depicting the goddess Srikandi in batik designs in the guise of the goddess of the Indonesian Women's Movement, Gerwani. In other batiks, the Javanese *banteng*, the wild ox—the chief symbol of Indonesian nationalism during colonial times—is included. Other of his designs included motifs from both Javanese and Chinese culture, expressing the unity of Indonesian peoples, or motifs speaking of the life of the peasant farmer and the needs of the common people, such as the cotton boll and rice stalks. While Hadi always worked within the classical idiom,

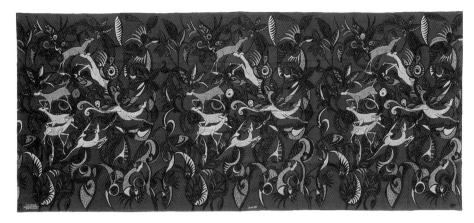

Some batik works have a dual purpose—as a wall hanging or as clothing. This piece was designed by C.V. Soemihardjo and made in 1996. 102 x 240 cm. (Willach collection)

A modern art form

It was in the 1970s that batik really took off as an art form, as artists developed the ideas introduced through the Batik Research Centre initiative of the previous decade. In 1970 Bagong Kussudiardja had established the Sanggar Banjar Barong, a studio workshop focused entirely on batik. At first there were many elements connecting the new works with both batik tradition and artistic traditions of the past. For example, although they moved away from the old symbolic meanings and the motifs which had been used to embellish the *sarung* and *kain* of the aristocracy, artists did not let go of the deeply rooted traditions of Indonesian art. The depiction of *topeng* (masks) drew on centuries of experience in which the peoples of Indonesia had carved and painted masks to be worn to scare away demons in dance and thus protect the community from malevolent forces. At the same time, the influence of batik tradition was still evident. Many of Bagong Kussudiardja's batik paintings reveal clearly the work of the *canting*, with the distinctive quality of the waxed line immediately apparent against the dark backgrounds. Some of his work borrows elements from the practice of *isen*, once painstakingly drawn and dotted behind and between the design elements by aristocratic ladies and their counterparts in the countryside. Parallel rows of arrows and waves, areas filled with spirals or fish-scale motifs (*gringsing*) evoke the long history of batik in Java, and the creamy golden ground against which the designs stand out recall the tree bark infusions which gave traditional batiks in Central Java their characteristic glow.

Abas Alibasyah was another batik artist producing work in the 1970s. He had been one of the already practising artists invited to take part in the Batik Research Centre project, and was one of the first to explore abstract expression through batik. In his batik works he often employed the dark sombre browns and blacks of traditional Central Javanese batik, but his themes could not be further away from that tradition. With the influence of his involvement in ASRI clearly

these subtle changes marked a radical departure in the way batik design was seen.

The legacy of the revolutionary ideology of Lekra was far-reaching, though the link with communism was short-lived. In the mid 1960s came a violent rejection of communism and a new regime looking for a third way, aligned with neither the Communist bloc nor the West. These political developments were reflected in the debate about what the role of art should be. Within communism, art was seen as a social tool to be used to further revolutionary aims, and much of the early art of the republic reflected this. Later, as Indonesia began to establish herself as a fully fledged nation, a more important issue was how far art could be used to express the national identity. In the case of Indonesia, the problem would be how to express an artistic unity in a state made up of so many different ethnic groups scattered throughout the archipelago. In this context, batik was able to claim a particular place. As a technique associated by now in the minds of the Javanese as a truly Indonesian craft, batik could be employed to express ideas without following Western models. At the same time, the use of a distinctively local medium would allow artists to explore notions which were the preoccupation of modern artists throughout the world. Although the techniques of batik were difficult for many artists to master, some took it up with enthusiasm, either specializing exclusively in batik or adding it to their artistic armoury. Others concentrated on design, employing specialists who could both apply the wax and undertake the dyeing.

evident, his work explored the abstract arrangement of shapes as well as representing so-called 'primitive' masks which gave his work a distinctly Indonesian intensity.

Batik painting developed rapidly during the 1970s, as did modern art in Indonesia generally. In 1975 an exhibition was held at Taman Ismail Marzuki Arts Centre in Jakarta entitled 'Gerakan Seni Rupa Baru Indonesia' (The New Arts Movement of Indonesia). The movement of the same name, which was launched at this exhibition, brought together a group of young artists who aimed to challenge the established artistic elite, in terms of both content and form. Their intention was to push back the boundaries of the art world, opening up the field to artists who wanted to use art as a means to explore contemporary social issues. Where art had come to be seen as the product of individual genius, a mystical expression of spiritual experience, those in the New Arts Movement of Indonesia wanted to break free from the constraints of conventional materials, subject matter and style. The old definition of fine arts as referring only to sculpture, painting and the graphic arts was regarded as insufficient and outmoded. More and more young artists started to include batik as part of their repertoire.

Responses to the inclusion of batik as an appropriate medium for artistic expression were varied. From many established artists there was some scepticism. Batik could not be regarded as equivalent to painting, and the medium was regarded as severely limited. However, as an art form among others, batik had much to offer. For artists whose work depended on quality of line, batik was an expressive and versatile medium. Though the line would necessarily be negative, light against dark, and the range of textural impression which could be achieved was regarded as narrow, batik made possible wholly new visual qualities which were free from the associations and traditions of other art forms.

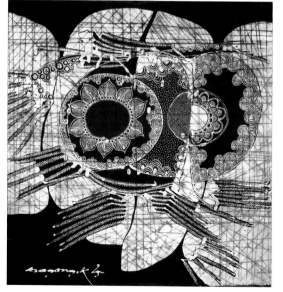

Untitled, Bagong Kussudiardja, 1975. 47 x 48 cm. (Smend collection)

Inspirations and approaches

The new artists obtained their inspiration from a range of sources. Many showed evidence of an awareness of forms which had only recently been introduced to Western art. Where earlier in the century many Western artists had been influenced by non-Western 'primitive' art, Indonesian artists in turn began to draw on such forms. The simple strong forms of the figures in the work of Damas exemplify this kind of subject and style.

Some batik artists working in the traditional *kain panjang* form continued to break new ground. Hardjonagoro had first broken down distinctions between court and coastal batik in a new national batik style in the 1950s. Having experimented with bold new colours in combination with classic designs and later with new motifs of his own, by the 1990s he had returned to the indigo and *soga* of courtly batik. Hardjonagoro continues to create new designs in response to changes in society, while remaining in the classical idiom, expressing meaning through symbolic motifs in traditional batik forms.

Most batik artists, however, drew on the forms of fine art painting in their batik work. Ida Hadjar is one whose distinctive style means that paintings resemble one another whether they are in oil or in batik. The simple solid shapes and rich colours of the human figures, with their smooth limbs and their outlines defined and emphasized with a solid black line, bring to mind the early work of Picasso and Matisse. The relationships between the figures suggest a narrative, albeit stylised and posed. Here too, there are echoes of the traditional batik maker's craft in the filling in of spaces with even-sized *isen* motifs.

The work of Mahyar, however, exploits all the possibilities of the batik technique to produce work which could be in no other medium. The stylized and simplified form of Mahyar's Bouraq is ornamented with jewellery, the sky, wings and tail embellished with naïve and colourful decorative motifs. These are characteristically simple, leaving the surface appearance almost flat, the only sense of depth provided by the overlapping contours of the hills, the staggered heights of the trees and the variously sized and coloured planets which recede into the darkness. It is a typically deceptive work, superficially child-like but evoking an underlying sense of the supernatural. The Bouraq is the creature which bore the prophet Mohammed to heaven on its back, and this work speaks clearly of Islam. However the subjects of most batik paintings are secular, and few have dealt with overtly religious subjects. One exception is Amri Yahya, whose works do on occasion include expressions of devotion to Islam.

Amri Yahya works in a range of media, including batik, which he has described as 'the people's spirit'. The colour and compositions of his oil paintings are reflected in his batik works, of which there are a prodigious number. For these, like many other artists, he paints his designs on paper and has them translated into batik by workers skilled in the medium. Much of his work is abstract in form—flat areas contrasting with areas where the evidence of the work of the wax is clear. Always the figures are clear and sharp. Amri's early landscapes have been widely imitated, though few have been able to suggest the feeling for the environment which comes through in his work.

Artists such as Tulus Warsito and Ahmad Sopandi drew on Amri's modernist approach to batik painting and developed the art in a new direction. Tulus Warsito works on fabric, but has broken from the conventional use of batik to define a flat two-dimensional space. Through the use of perspective, shadows and other devices, he creates an illusion not just of depth, but of air, even in abstract forms. Objects and shapes float in space, defying the surface of the painting. Evidence of the use of the *canting* is far less prevalent in Tulus' work than in those of other batik artists. Despite his revolutionary approach to batik work, a result of playful experimentation as a young man, he still sometimes draws his inspiration from traditional motifs, mobilizing symbols which resonate throughout Indonesian art. Thus his batik painting *View through a Window* evokes the image of the mountain, a reference to Mount Meru, so long at the centre of Indonesian cosmological belief as the birthplace of the gods.

Other artists have pushed back the boundaries of batik. Ardiyanto Pranata's inventive use of textile forms, for example,

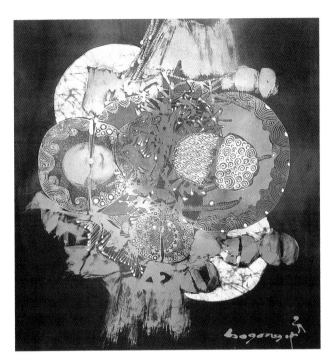

Composition, Bagong Kussudiardja, 1973. 44.5 x 44.5 cm. (Smend collection)

sometimes results in the batik elements becoming part of a three-dimensional textile construction in which quilting, appliqué and other devices play a part. Nia Fliam and Agus Ismoyo, on the other hand, combine traditional elements with modern design to produce vibrant images which have movement, light and depth.

Contemporary developments

The subjects and styles of batik paintings have been affected by demand from both local and overseas purchasers. This is especially true of paintings for the tourist market, but also for works destined for the international art market. A number of schools of artists have emerged, some favouring images of the Javanese landscape, others depicting figures from shadow theatre (*wayang*) stories or images associated with other parts of Indonesia. Paintings in surrealist styles continue to find favour, and many of the paintings made famous in the 1970s still serve as models for the less inventive. Nevertheless, batik artists in Yogyakarta and elsewhere continue to experiment with subject matter, colour, shape and line and the lively and creative art form spawned after independence continues to produce new and vibrant works.

OPPOSITE: *Two Figures*,
Bagong Kussudiardja, 1973.
45.5 x 50 cm. (Smend collection)

ABOVE: *Bouraq*, Mahyar, 1976.
47 x 53 cm. (Smend collection)

Scene with Women in Bali,
Ida Hadjar, 1992. 94 x 128 cm.
(Willach collection)

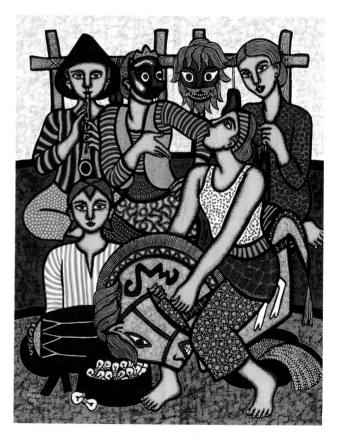

Scene with Horse Dancer, Wayang
Topeng *and* Gamelan *Musicians,*
Ida Hadjar, 1994.
94 x 128 cm. (Willach collection)

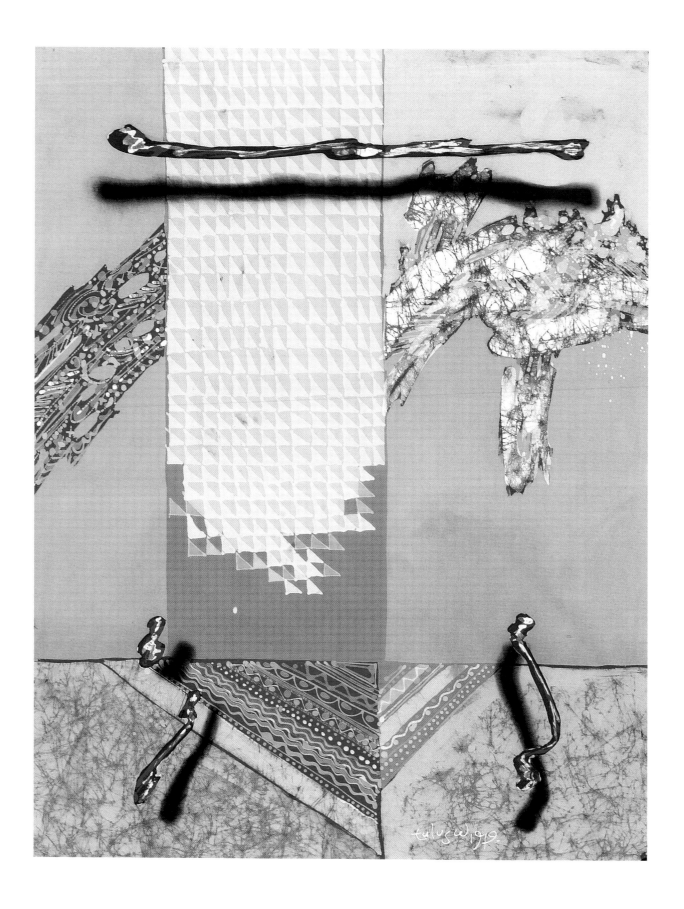

OPPOSITE: *Composition*,
Tulus Warsito, 1979.
73 x 94 cm. (Smend collection)

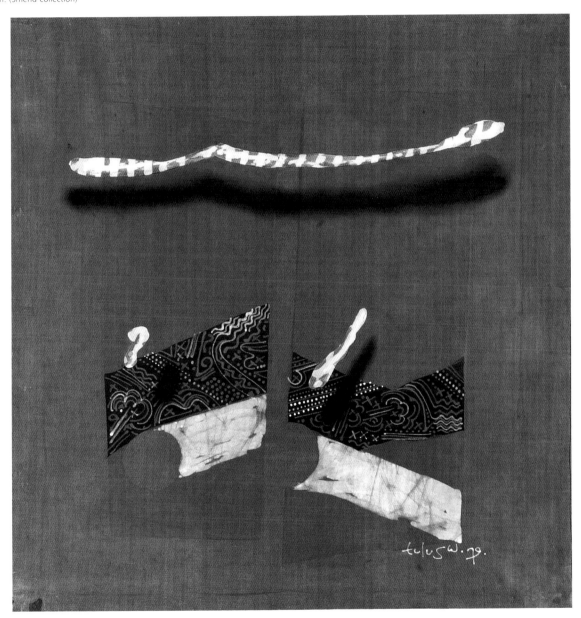

View from a Window,
Tulus Warsito, 1979.
48.5 x 49.5 cm. (Smend collection)

BELOW: *Landscape*,
Amri Yahya, 1974.
35.5 x 37.5 cm. (Smend collection)

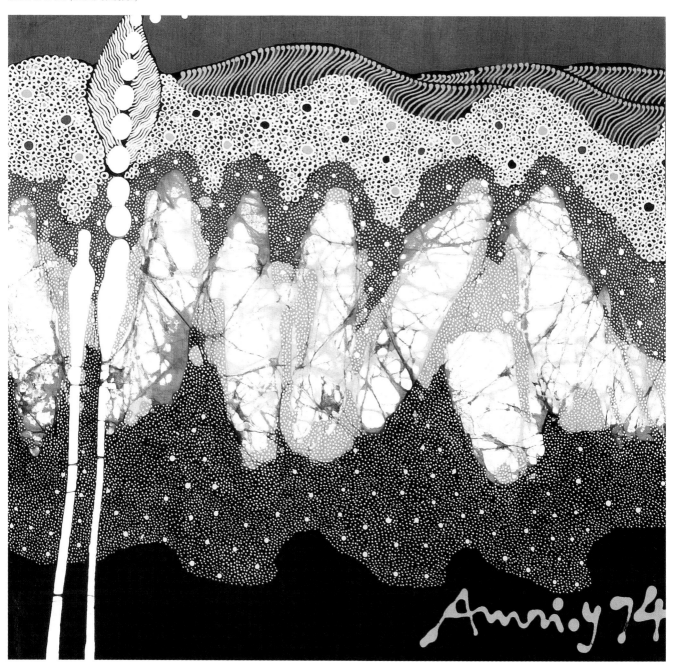

OPPOSITE: *House with Two Birds*,
Ardiyanto Pranata, 1998.
33 x 51 cm. (Smend collection)

LEFT TOP: *Sekar Jagad* (Flowers of the World), Agus Ismoyo, Nia Fliam, 1995. 115 x 250 cm (Museum and Art Gallery of the Northern Territory, Darwin. IND 02006)

LEFT BOTTOM: *Kain Doa* (Prayer Cloth), Agus Ismoyo, Nia Fliam, 2004. 60 x 210 cm (Museum and Art Gallery of the Northern Territory, Darwin. IND 02946)

ABOVE: Deer-hunting scene by
Ardiyanto Pranata.
Tulis, cotton. (Courtesy of the
Italian ambassador to Turkey,
His Excellency Dr. Carlo Marsili
and his wife Mme Marsili)

FOLLOWING PAGES: Stylized *parang*
design from the workshop of
The Tjien Sing of Yogyakarta.
Tulis, cotton. Before 1928.
106.5 x 246 cm.
(Smend collection)

Glossary

A

abaca *(Musa textilis)* – a kind of banana plantain whose leaf stems provide a fibre used for weaving especially in the Philippines

alas-alasan – 'forest' pattern on batik cloth

B

bangun tulak – lit. 'to repel misfortune'. Phrase used in descriptions or names of cloths with an apotropaic (preventing evil) function

bedoyo – slow ceremonial court dance from the Central Javanese *kraton* (qv); usually performed by nine female dancers

C

cambric – fine white cotton cloth

canting (pronounced 'chunting') – pen-like instrument consisting of a stem, usually bamboo, and a copper bowl with a spout through which hot wax is drawn on the cloth

cap (pronounced 'chup') – stamp, usually of copper strips soldered together in the shape of a motif, with which hot wax is impressed onto the cloth

complongan (pronounced 'chomplongan') – tool used in batik making to prick holes in a layer of wax to allow dye to penetrate, resulting in dots on the finished cloth

D/G

dodot – exceptionally large cloth, normally formed from two widths of cloth joined together at the selvedges, and worn by members of the nobility, court dancers and brides and grooms on their wedding day

gendongan – cloth used for carrying babies especially in Java

I

ikat – lit. 'to tie'. A textile patterning technique in which the warp threads are tied in order to resist the dyebath before weaving, thus producing a pattern in the finished cloth

iket kepala – man's headcloth

isen – filling designs used to decorate the background areas of a batik cloth

J

jirak (Symplocos fasciculata) – a plant rich in aluminium, used in combination with *mengkudu* (qv) as a mordant

jumputan – method of creating patterns in a cloth by tying or sewing and gathering the cloth before dyeing

K

kain – colloquial term for *kain panjang* (qv)

kain panjang – wide skirt cloth used especially on formal occasions

kain simbut – ritual cloths used in parts of Sunda, West Java, produced using a rice-paste resist method

kebaya – long fitted blouse, often of lacy or fine fabric, worn especially by Javanese women

kemben – cloth used for wrapping around the breast, especially by court dancers and brides in traditional Javanese costume

kepala – part of a *sarung*, normally one-third of its width, usually containing the triangular *tumpal* design

kraton – palace, especially in Java

L

larangan – lit. 'forbidden'. A term used to refer to motifs whose use was restricted to the sultan and members of his family

lokcan (pronounced 'lokchun') – style of batik patterning, usually on silk, with animal and bird designs originating from Chinese iconography. The word derives from the Chinese term for 'blue silk', suggesting the design was originally in blue, though it occurs more commonly in brown

M

Mataram – Central Javanese state which came to power in the late 16th century, splitting in two in 1755 with capitals at Yogyakarta and Surakarta (present-day Solo)

mengkudu (Morinda citrifolia) – the morinda tree, whose root yields a red dye

mordant – a substance used to help 'bind' a dye to the cloth

P

papan – vertical panels on either side of the *kepala* (qv) of a *sarung*

patola (plural *patolu*) – silk cloth from India made in the double-*ikat* technique whereby both warp and weft threads were tied before dyeing to create a resist pattern in the cloth

perada – method of applying gold patterning to cloth in the form of dust, gold leaf or, nowadays, paint

R

raden, raden mas – title accorded to members of the nobility of a certain rank, especially in Java

ramie *(Boehmeria nivea)* – shrub whose stem provides a strong fibre used for weaving, especially in the Philippines

S

sampur – a long narrow cloth worn as a sash by dancers and incorporated into the dance movements

sarung – skirt cloth sewn into a tube

sawat – motif resembling two wings and a tail feather, said to represent Garuda, the man-eagle mount of a central Hindu deity, Vishnu

semen – batik patterns consisting of curling shoots of young foliage

serimpi – Central Javanese court dance performed by four female dancers representing the four elements of earth, air, fire and water

sido mukti – lit. 'wish for prosperity'. A class of motifs in a lattice design

soga – sombre brown dye produced by the bark of certain trees

songket – brocade using metallic threads; the technique of weaving with such threads as supplementary weft, usually on a silk ground

T

tritik – 'thread resist' technique in which patterns are made by stitching and gathering the cloth before dyeing

tulis – lit. 'to write'. *Batik tulis* is hand-drawn batik produced with the use of the *canting* (qv)

tumpal – the part of the *kepala* (qv) of a batik cloth decorated with rows of opposing triangles

W

warp ikat – the technique of producing a pattern on a woven cloth by tying the warp threads before dyeing

Map of Batik-producing Areas

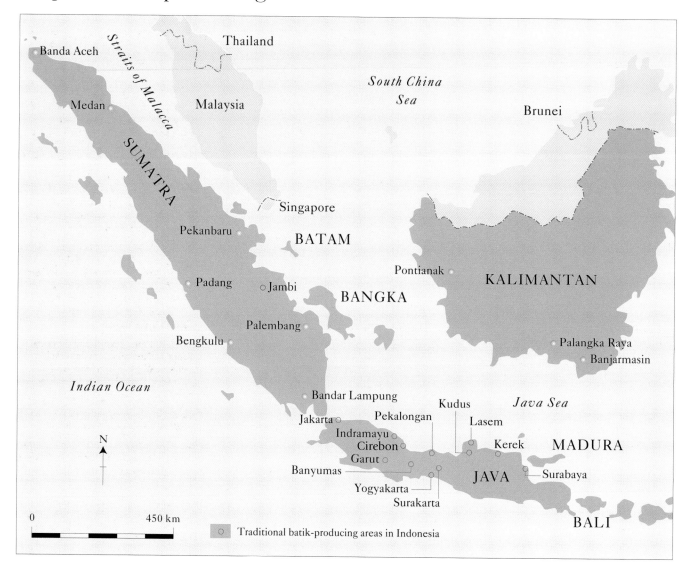

Traditional batik-producing areas in Indonesia

Bibliography

Abdurachman, P. R. 1982. 'Tradisi Batik Cirebon' in P. R. Abdurachman (ed.) *Cerbon*. Jakarta: Yayasan Mitra Budayan and Sinar Harapan. pp. 129–57.

Abdurachman, P. R. 1987. 'Dermayu Batiks: A Surviving Art in an Ancient Trading Town'. *SPAFA Digest*. Volume 8, no. 1. pp. 3–8.

Achjadi, J. 1989. 'Batiks in the Central Javanese Wedding Ceremony' in M. Gittinger (ed.) *To Speak With Cloth: Studies in Indonesian Textiles*. Los Angeles: Museum of Cultural History, University of California. pp. 151–61.

Achjadi, J. (ed.) 1999. *Batik: Spirit of Indonesia*. Jakarta and Singapore: Yayasan Batik Indonesia, PT Buku Antar Bangsa and Editions Didier Millet.

Adam, T. 1934. 'The Art of Batik in Java'. *Bulletin of the Needle and Bobbin Club*. Volume 18, no. 1–2. pp. 1–79.

Adams, M. 1970. 'Symbolic Scenes in Javanese Batik'. *Textile Museum Journal*. Volume 3, no. 1. pp. 25–40.

Arensberg, S. M. 1978. *Javanese Batiks*. Boston: Museum of Fine Arts.

Bintarto, Hardjosuwinjo. 1958. 'The Batik Industry in Central Java'. *Ekonomi dan Keuangan Indonesia*. Volume 11, no. 7. pp. 345–401.

Boow, J. 1989. *Symbol and Status in Javanese Batik*. Asian Studies Centre Monograph Series, no. 7. Nedlands: University of Western Australia.

Brenner, S. A. 1998. *The Domestication of Desire: Women, Wealth and Modernity in Java*. Princeton, New Jersey: Princeton University Press.

Cammann, S. 1953. 'Types of Symbols in Chinese Art' in A. F. Wright (ed.) *Studies in Chinese Thought*. Chicago: University of Chicago Press.

Christie, J. W. 1993. 'Texts and Textiles in Medieval Java'. *Bulletin de l'École Française d'Extrême-Orient*. Volume 80, no. 1. pp. 181–211.

Daubanton, J. D. 1922. *Beknopte Beschrijving van de Batikindustrie op Java Haar Onstaan en Ontwikkeling, Bewerking der Goederen, Gebruikte Materialen en Voorbrengselen*. Rotterdam.

De Kat Angelino, P. 1930. *Batikrapport*. Weltvreden: Kantoor van Arbeid.

Djoemena, N. S. 1986. *Ungkapan Sehelai Batik: Its Mystery and Meaning*. Jakarta: Penerbit Djambatan.

Djoemena, N. S. 1991. *Batik dan Mitra: Batik and Its Kind*. Jakarta: Penerbit Djambatan.

Djoemena, N. S. 1993. 'Batik Treasures of the Special Region of Yogyakarta' in M. Nabholz-Kartaschoff et al. (eds.) *Weaving Patterns of Life*. Basel: Museum of Ethnography. pp. 433–48.

Donahue, L. O. 1982. *Encyclopaedia of Batik Design*. East Brunswick: Associated Universities Press.

Duggan, G. 2001. 'The Chinese Batiks of Java' in Itie van Hout (ed.) *Batik Drawn in Wax: 200 Years of Batik Art from Indonesia in the Tropenmuseum Collection*. Amsterdam: Royal Tropical Institute. pp. 90–105.

Elliott, I. M. 1984. *Batik: Fabled Cloth of Java*. New York: Clarkson & Potter.

Forge, A. 1989. 'Batik Patterns of the Early Nineteenth Century' in M. Gittinger (ed.) *To Speak with Cloth: Studies in Indonesian Textiles*. Los Angeles: Museum of Cultural History, University of California. pp. 91–105.

Fraser-Lu, S. 1986. *Indonesian Batik: Processes, Patterns and Places*. Singapore: Oxford University Press.

Furnivall, J. S. 1936. 'The Weaving and Batik Industries in Java'. *Asiatic Review*. Volume 32, no. 3 (April).

Geirnaert, D. C. and R. Heringa. 1989. *The A.E.D.T.A. Batik Collection*. Paris: Association pour l'Étude et la Documentation des Textiles d'Asie.

Geirnaert-Martin, D. 1983. 'Ask Lurik Why Batik: A Structural Analysis of Textiles and Classifications (Central Java)' in J. G. Oosten and A. de Ruijter (eds.) *The Future of Structuralism*. Papers of IUAES Intercongress, Amsterdam 1981. pp. 155–99.

Gittinger, M. 1979. *Splendid Symbols: Textiles and Tradition in Indonesia*. Singapore: Oxford University Press.

Gittinger, M. (ed.) 1980. *Indonesian Textiles: Irene Emery Roundtable on Museum Textiles*. Washington, D.C.: The Textile Museum.

Gittinger, M. (ed.) 1989. *To Speak with Cloth: Studies in Indonesian Textiles*. Los Angeles: Museum of Cultural History, University of California.

Haake, A. 1984. *Javanische Batik: Methode, Symbolik, Geschichte*. Hannover: Schaper.

Hafsah, Asah. 1973. *Seni Batik Tradisional Desa Trusmi Kabupaten Cirebon*. Thesis, Universitas Gajah Mada.

Hamzuri. 1981. *Batik Klasik/Classical Batik*. (English translation by Judi Achjadi). Jakarta: Djambatan.

Hardjonagoro, K. R. T. 1980. 'The Place of Batik in the History and Philosophy of Javanese Textiles: A Personal View', translated by R. J. Holmgren, in M. Gittinger (ed.) *Indonesian Textiles: Irene Emery Roundtable on Museum Textiles*. Washington, D.C.: The Textile Museum. pp. 223–42.

Hasanudin. 1974. *Batik Pekalongan, Sebuah Thesis Tentang Disain Batik Pekalongan*. Thesis, Institut Teknologi Bandung.

Hawkins, E. D. 1961. 'The Batik Industry: The Role of the Javanese Entrepreneur' in B. Higgins (ed.) *Entrepreneurship and Labor Skills in Indonesian Economic Development: A Symposium*. New Haven, Connecticut: Yale University Southeast Asian Studies Monograph no. 1. pp. 39–74.

Heringa, R. 1989. 'Javaanse katoentjes' in B. Brommer (ed.) *Katoendruk in Nederland*. Tilburg & Helmond: Nederlands Textielmuseum & Gemeentemuseum Helmond. pp. 135–56.

Heringa, R. 1989. 'Dye Process and Life Sequence: The Colouring of Textiles in an East Javanese Village' in M. Gittinger (ed.) *To Speak With Cloth: Studies in Indonesian Textiles*. Los Angeles: Museum of Cultural History, University of California. pp. 106–30.

Heringa, R. 1991. 'Textiles and the Social Fabric on Northeast Java' in G. Volger and K. v. Welck (eds.) *Indonesian Textiles Symposium 1985*. Cologne: Ethnologica. pp. 44–53.

Heringa, R. 1994. *Spiegels van ruimte en tijd: textile uit Tuban*. Den Haag: Museon.

Heringa, R. and H. Veldhuisen. (eds.) 1996. *Fabric of Enchantment: Batik from the North Coast of Java*. Los Angeles: Los Angeles County Museum of Art.

Hitchcock, M. and Wiendu Nuryanti. (eds.) 2000. *Building on Batik: The Globalization of A Craft Community*. Proceedings of the Dunia Batik Conference, Yogyakarta, Indonesia, 1997. Aldershot: Ashgate.

Jasper, J. E. and Mas Pirngadie. 1916. *De Inlandsche Kunstnijverheid in Nederlandsch Indie. Volume III De Batikkunst.* 's-Gravenhage.

Joseph, R. 1987. *Diffused Batik Production in Central Java.* PhD thesis. University of California, San Diego.

Joseph, R. 1987. *Worker, Middlewoman, Entrepreneur: Women in the Indonesian Batik Industry.* Bangkok: The Population Council.

Kahlenberg, M. H. 1980. 'The Influence of the European Herbal on Indonesian Batik' in M. Gittinger (ed.) *Indonesian Textiles: Irene Emery Roundtable on Museum Textiles.* Washington, D.C.: The Textile Museum. pp. 243–47.

Kajitani, Nobuko. 1980. 'Traditional Dyes in Indonesia' in M. Gittinger (ed.) *Indonesian Textiles: Irene Emery Roundtable on Museum Textiles.* Washington, D.C.: The Textile Museum. pp. 305–25.

Kats, J. 1922. 'De Achteruitgang van de Batikkunst'. *Djawa.* 2: 92–98.

Kerlogue, F. G. 1996. *Scattered Flowers: Batiks from Jambi, Sumatra.* Hull: University of Hull Press.

Kerlogue, F. G. 1999. 'Batik, The Cloth of Kings' in N. Barley (ed.) *The Golden Sword: Stamford Raffles and the East.* London: British Museum Press. pp. 30–35.

Kerlogue, F. G. 2001. 'The Batik of Madura' in Itie van Hout (ed.) *Batik Drawn in Wax: 200 Years of Batik Art from Indonesia in the Tropenmuseum Collection.* Amsterdam: Royal Tropical Institute. pp. 66–77.

Kerlogue, F. G. 2001. 'Islamic Talismans: The Calligraphy Batiks' in Itie van Hout (ed.) *Batik Drawn in Wax: 200 Years of Batik Art from Indonesia in the Tropenmuseum Collection.* Amsterdam: Royal Tropical Institute. pp. 124–35.

Kerlogue, F. G. 2001. 'Flowers, Fruits and Fragrance: The Batiks of Jambi' in Itie van Hout (ed.) *Batik Drawn in Wax: 200 Years of Batik Art from Indonesia in the Tropenmuseum Collection.* Amsterdam: Royal Tropical Institute. pp. 78–89.

Koperberg, S. 1922. 'De Javaansche Batikindustrie'. *Djawa.* 2: 147–56.

Krevitsky, N. 1964. *Batik: Art and Craft.* New York: Van Nostrand Reinhold.

Labin, B. 1979. 'Batik Traditions in the Life of the Javanese' in J. Fischer (ed.) *Threads of Tradition.* Berkeley: Lowie Museum of Anthropology. pp. 41–52.

Langewis, L. and F. A. Wagner. 1964. *Decorative Art in Indonesian Textiles.* Amsterdam: Van der Peet.

Larsen, J. L. et al. 1976. *The Dyer's Art: Ikat, Batik, Pelangi.* New York: Van Nostrand Reinhold.

Lewis, A. B. 1924. *Javanese Batik Designs from Metal Stamps.* Chicago: Field Museum of Natural History.

Loeber, J. A. 1926. *Das Batiken.* Oldenburg: Stalling.

Marhamah. 1993. *Batik Tradisional Jambi dan Perkembangannya.* Jambi: Kanwil Departemen Perindustrien Propinsi Jambi.

Marsden, W. [1811] 1986. *The History of Sumatra.* Reprint, with introduction by John Bastin. Singapore: Oxford University Press.

Matsuo, Horoshi. 1970. *The Development of the Javanese Cotton Industry.* Tokyo: Institute of Developing Economies, Occasional Series, no 7.

Maxwell, R. 1990. 'Southeast Asian Textiles: Japanese Influences on Javanese Batik'. *Australian National Gallery Association News.* July/August.

Maxwell, R. J. and J. R. Maxwell. 1989. 'Political Motives: The Batiks of Mohamad Hadi of Solo' in M. Gittinger (ed.) *To Speak With Cloth: Studies in Indonesian Textiles.* Los Angeles: Museum of Cultural History, University of California. pp. 131–50.

Nooy-Palm, H. 1980. 'The Role of the Sacred Cloths in the Mythology and Ritual of the Sa'dan Toraja of Sulawesi, Indonesia' in M. Gittinger (ed.) *Indonesian Textiles: Irene Emery Roundtable on Museum Textiles.* Washington, D.C.: The Textile Museum. pp. 81–95.

Palmier, L. H. 1961. 'Batik Manufacture in a Chinese Community in Java' in B. Higgins (ed.) *Entrepreneurship and Labor Skills in Indonesian Economic Development: A Symposium.* New Haven: Yale University Southeast Asian Studies Monograph no. 1. pp. 75–97.

Praetorius, C. F. E. 1843. 'Nijverheid in de hoofdplaats van Palembang'. *Indische bij Tijdschrift.* Volume 1. pp. 383–404.

Raadt-Apell, M. J. de. 1980. *De batikkerij van Zuylen te Pekalongan (Midden Java 1890–1946).* Uitgeverij Terra-Zutphen.

Raffles, T. S. [1817] 1965. *The History of Java.* Reprint. Kuala Lumpur: Oxford University Press.

Rouffaer, G. P. and H. H. Juynboll. 1914. *De Batikkunst in Nederlandsch-Indie en Haar Geschiedenis.* Utrecht: Oosthoek.

Soetopo, S. 1957. 'Batic' in *Education and Culture.* Number 9. Jakarta: Ministry of Education, Instruction and Culture.

Solyom, G. and B. Solyom. 1980. 'Cosmic Symbolism in Semen and Alasalasan Patterns in Javanese Textiles' in M. Gittinger (ed.) *Indonesian Textiles: Irene Emery Roundtable on Museum Textiles.* Washington, D.C.: The Textile Museum. pp. 248–63.

Steinmann, A. 1947. 'The Art of Batik'. *Ciba Review.* Volume 58, pp. 2090–101.

Steinmann, A. 1947. 'Batik Work, Its Origin and Spread.' *Ciba Review.* Volume 58, pp. 2102–09.

Steinmann, A. 1947. 'Batik Designs'. *Ciba Review.* Volume 58, pp. 2110–28.

Susanto, S. K. S. 1980. *Seni Kerajinan Batik Indonesia.* Yogyakarta: Balai Penelitian Batik dan Kerajinan.

Tirtaamidjaja, N. 1966. *Batik: Pola dan Tjorak.* Jakarta: Penerbit Djambatan.

Van Dijk, K. 1997. 'Sarong, Jubbah and Trousers: Appearance as Means of Distinction and Discrimination' in H. S. Nordholt (ed.) *Outward Appearances: Dressing, State and Society in Indonesia.* Leiden: KITLV.

Veldhuisen, H. 1993. *Batik Belanda 1840–1940: Dutch Influence on Batik from Java, History and Stories.* Jakarta: Gaya Favorit Press.

Veldhuisen-Djajasoebrata, A. 1980. 'On the Origin and Nature of Larangan: Forbidden Batik Patterns from the Central Javanese Principalities' in M. Gittinger (ed.) *Indonesian Textiles: Irene Emery Roundtable on Museum Textiles.* Washington, D.C.: The Textile Museum. pp. 201–42.

Veldhuisen-Djajasoebrata, A. 1984. *Bloemen van het Heelal.* Rotterdam: Museum voor Land- en Volkenkunde.

Vuldy, C. 1991. 'Pekalongan as a Center of Batik Trade' in G. Volger and K. v. Welck (eds.) *Indonesian Textiles Symposium 1985,* Cologne: Rautenstrauch-Joest-Museum/ Ethnologica. pp. 171–73.

Warming, W. and M. Gaworski. 1981. *The World of Indonesian Textiles.* Tokyo: Kodansha.

Wirodihardjo, Dr Saraso. 1954. *Ko-operasi dan Masalah Batik.* Jakarta: Gabungan Ko-operasi Batik Indonesia.

Index

Note: Numbers in italics refer to illustrations.

Acknowledgements

The author and publisher would like to thank the individuals and organizations whose photographs are reproduced in this book.

All photographs, apart from the following, were taken by Fulvio Zanettini.

Yu-Chee Chong Fine Art, London: 32, 93(l), 142, 143(b), 192
Editions Didier Millet archives: 19, 24, 25(r), 26(r), 27, 76
Haks and Maris, Amsterdam: 148(l), 149(r), 151(t)
Hull University Photographic Service: 4–5, 12, 30, 35, 41(t), 42(t), 51(t), 61, 64, 71(t), 94, 95
Leo Haks photo collection, Amsterdam: 2, 13, 39, 134, 137, 138, 140, 141, 143(t), 144, 145, 146, 147, 148(r), 149(l), 150
Agus Ismoyo and Nia Fliam: 180(t), 180(b)
Chris Raab (Museon, The Hague): 52, 53
Tara Sosrowardoyo: 11, 25(l), 181
Luca Invernizzi Tettoni: 151(b)
Courtesy of Tropenmuseum, Amsterdam: 59(b)
Wereldmuseum, Rotterdam: 23(b)

Numbers refer to page numbers. Letters refer to position:
(l) left; (r) right; (t) top; (b) bottom.

Thank you also to the following for giving permission for their batiks and images to be included in the book:

Fiona Kerlogue
Brigitte Willach (www.willach-atelier.de)
Leo Haks and Guus Maris (www.leohaks.com)
Yu-Chee Chong
Agus Ismoyo and Nia Fliam
His Excellency Dr. Carlo Marsili and Mme Marsili
Museon, The Hague
Museum and Art Gallery of the Northern Territory, Darwin
Tropenmuseum, Amsterdam
Wereldmuseum, Rotterdam

Particular thanks are due to Rudolf G. Smend, whose collection provided the vast majority of the illustrations for this book.

Galerie Smend
Mainzer Str. 31
50678 Köln
Germany
Tel.: +49.221.31 20 47 Fax: +49.221.9 32 07 18
E-mail: smend@smend.de Web: www.smend.de
See also: Smend, Rudolf G., Harper, Donald J. 2004. *Batik: From the Courts of Java and Sumatra*. Singapore: Periplus Editions, 2004. Published in the USA by Tuttle Publishing, 2004.

Javanese chief. Photograph by Isidore van Kinsbergen, 1865–68.
(Yu-Chee Chong Fine Art, London)

Museum Collections of Batik

INDONESIA
Museum Tekstil, Jakarta
Museum Nasional, Jakarta
Museum Radya Pustaka
Museum Sono Budoyo
Museum Ullen Sentalu
Museum Negeri Propinsi Jambi

AUSTRALIA
Australian National Gallery, Canberra

AUSTRIA
Museum für Völkerkunde, Vienna
Koninklijke Museum voor Kunst en Geschiedenis, Vienna

CANADA
Royal Ontario Museum, Toronto
Textile Museum of Canada, Toronto

DENMARK
National Museum of Denmark, Copenhagen

GERMANY
Museum für Völkerkunde, Berlin
Museum für Völkerkunde, Frankfurt
Staatliches Museum für Völkerkunde, München
Ethnography Museum, Leipzig
Rautenstrauch-Joest Museum für Völkerkunde, Köln
Deutsches Textilmuseum Krefeld, Köln

FRANCE
Musée de l'Homme, Paris

JAPAN
Fukuoka Art Museum, Fukuoka
National Museum of Ethnology, Osaka
Tokyo National Museum, Tokyo

MALAYSIA
Muzium Seni Asia, Universiti Malaya, Kuala Lumpur
National Art Gallery, Kuala Lumpur
National Museum, Kuala Lumpur

THE NETHERLANDS
Museum voor Land- en Volkenkunde, Rotterdam
Volkenkundig Museum Nusantara, Delft
Tropenmuseum, Amsterdam
Museum voor het Onderwijs/Museon, The Hague
Rijksmuseum voor Volkenkunde, Leiden
Nederlands Textielmuseum, Tilburg

SINGAPORE
Asian Civilisations Museum, Singapore

SWEDEN
Ethnographical Museum of Sweden, Stockholm

SWITZERLAND
Museum für Völkerkunde, Basel
Bernisches Historisches Museum, Bern
Musée d'Ethnographie de Genève, Geneva
Musée d'Ethnographie de Neuchâtel
Bellerive Museum of Zurich
Völkerkundemuseum der Universität Zurich

UNITED KINGDOM
Victoria and Albert Museum, London
Museum of Mankind, London
Pitt Rivers Museum, Oxford
Southeast Asia Museum, University of Hull
National Museum of Scotland, Edinburgh
Horniman Museum, London

USA
American Museum of Natural History, New York
Boston Museum of Fine Arts, Boston
The Brooklyn Museum, New York
Cooper-Hewitt Museum of Design, New York
Field Museum of Natural History, Chicago
Fowler Museum of Cultural History, University of California, Los Angeles
Los Angeles County Museum of Art
Metropolitan Museum of Art, New York
The Minneapolis Institute of Arts
The Museum of International Folk Art, Santa Fe
The National Museum of American History, Washington, D.C.
Peabody Museum of Salem
The Textile Museum, Washington, D.C.
The University Museum, Philadelphia